The

MAGIC

MONEY

MACHINE

*An Introduction to Personal Finance;
Be Prepared and Achieve Financial
Security*

Marvin L. Piersall

ISBN: 149918980X
ISBN 13: 9781499189803

Library of Congress Control Number: 2014907392
CreateSpace Independent Publishing Platform
North Charleston, South Carolina

*This book is dedicated to all who answered the call to arms
and their loved ones who welcomed them home.*

CONTENTS

FOREWORD

It was a beautiful day, and my twenty-eight-year-old son was helping me put in a garden. Sweat and hard work reminded me of the old saying "Your money either works for you, or you work for your money!" I shared it, and he said, "Dad, I think you should write a book for people like me and my friends."

"What do you mean by that?"

"Oh, you know, for people who do 'real work' for a living, not sit around and play on a computer."

"What should the book be about?"

"It should be about the investment stuff you talk about all the time. It should be simple and have everything you need to know, all in one place, so people could understand it."

Later in the day, I mentioned something Benjamin Graham said, and my son said, "See what I'm talking about! No one has ever heard of Benjamin Graham, none of my friends! Who is Benjamin Graham?"

I said, "He wrote a famous book on security analysis and is often quoted by value investors."

I think I got his point. People have different gifts, talents, training, experience, and interests. I recalled teaching a doctor how to read a stock page in *The Wall Street Journal* some thirty years ago. His background was biology, science, and medicine. I don't think he had any finance or business training. In fact, many people have little training or education in this area. My son now has a start.

It is difficult to get simple, straightforward, honest, and unbiased information when one is researching anything, let alone investing. Often those "teaching" investments are getting paid to sell insurance, warranties, or financial and loan products. People who do not understand the basics of personal finance are less able to make wise choices and can end up with poor products. The result is that many won't be able to retire on time, let alone early. A serious mistake can mean having to work until your health is gone, and it's too late to enjoy life.

My son is not the first (or even the second or third) person to suggest that I write a book to help people with their money issues. Perhaps regular working people would read a short, simple book that explained the basics of personal finance if they knew it could help them retire five, ten, or even twenty years sooner than they thought possible. Could such a book help set people, such as my son, on the path to financial success and a good retirement while they are still young and healthy enough to enjoy it? What do you think?

ACKNOWLEDGEMENTS

I want to thank coworkers and friends who, throughout the years, have suggested that I write a book to help people with their personal finances. They planted the initial seeds. I especially want to thank my sister Sherry Connelly, brother Gary, sister-in-law Rhonda, daughter Mary, son Matt, step-mom Lola, and my dad George without who's interest, encouragement, and support, this book would not have been written or published.

I also feel a deep sense of gratitude to my dear, departed mother Marilyn (Battershell) Piersall for teaching me how to read before I started school and for her consistent demonstrations of love, faith, and integrity. I am forever grateful.

INTRODUCTION

My introduction to investing and research happened when I was a young boy investing in silver coins. As you may be aware, silver coins produced prior to 1965 were 90 percent silver. Dimes, quarters, and half dollars produced in 1965 and in later years were mostly copper. My research indicated I should concentrate on silver coins produced prior to 1965. I still have them. Some of the coins are now worth forty to fifty times what I paid for them. The only problem is they do not provide income or reduce my expenses.

As it is with all collectibles, such as art, antiques, baseball cards, and coins, the only way to get money out of them is to sell them. Because I've had the coins since I was a boy, and some are from my parents and grandparents, I don't want to sell them. What I need is something that makes coins, so I can spend them: a magic money machine!

Chapter 1

THE DANCE

It's a nice evening, and I'm meeting some friends at a charity dance. I understand there is going to be an auction and magic show. It's for a good cause, and I'm looking forward to it.

Ronald McDonald House Charities is a real help for people when the chips are down. That's where I met Tom, who was laid off a few weeks after he found out his wife was pregnant. The tire plant had closed, and he was unable to find a job with benefits, so he took a job at a local tire shop. It wasn't as much money, but over three hundred people had lost their jobs, so he was thankful. He hoped they could hang on to the home they purchased a couple of years ago, but didn't know if that would be possible. Their baby was born with some problems and had to have an expensive, life-saving surgery.

Ronald McDonald House Charities provides a place to stay for parents, so they can be near where their children are hospitalized. Since Tom and his wife lived about an hour and a half away, this was a real blessing. His wife was there during the week, and he came over on the weekends after he got off work. The parents usually came back from the hospital later in the evening after the nurses had kicked them out. The local churches helped out by providing meals, clean up, and sympathetic ears. That's where I came in. I did not mind taking food there or giving some of my time. I have found you meet some of the nicest people doing volunteer work.

It's a little noisy but not too bad, and I see some people I know. What was that word I just heard from Marge, the local Ronald McDonald House Charities manager? Did I hear *widget*? I haven't heard that word in a long time. It is a term well known to every business major. It is defined by *Webster's Dictionary* as a gadget or unnamed article considered for purposes of hypothetical example. I think of it as a pretend product college professors use in teaching. What is the announcer saying? They are going to auction off widgets that produce two quarters per month.

I wonder what in the world they are auctioning that produces fifty cents per month or six dollars per year. What machines produce quarters other than the government mint and parking meters? Laundromat machines and coin-operated pool tables come to mind. Now that I think of it, basically any type of vending machine will bring in quarters, but I'm sure they all bring in much more than fifty cents per month. Maybe they are doing something like buying a Laundromat machine for the shelter, and everyone will get back fifty cents per month.

Maybe it's not a machine. Could it be some type of plant that produces fruit worth fifty cents per month? Perhaps it's a share of an animal like a cow or chicken that produces milk or eggs worth fifty cents per month. Maybe we are all chipping in on a new or expanded shelter, and we each get fifty cents per month back. I can't imagine what would produce fifty cents per month. I have a few questions to ask before I can place a value on the fifty-cent-per-month income.

Meanwhile, I hear some good old rock 'n' roll swing dance music. It is a good time to hit the dance floor.

Chapter 2

THE SLOW DANCE

I'm glad we're getting to have a slow dance, because it gives me a chance to think and slow my heart rate. Swing and salsa require more concentration and physical effort. Dancing reminds me of sailing. Both activities require the use of both sides of my brain simultaneously.

In fact, I was introduced to sailing and investing for income simultaneously. A couple of my shipmates from Helicopter Combat Support Squadron Three and I rented a condo off of our base, Naval Air Station North Island. We were living across from the marina, and there I met a forty-year-old investor, who had a major impact on my life, and he was the reason I started buying rental properties as soon as I was discharged and got home. He had retired and was always scuba diving or sailing off to exotic places like Hawaii. I had never heard of anyone that young escaping wage servitude and being free to enjoy life to its fullest. Everyone I knew back home in Illinois worked until they were well on in years or had lost their health. Ever since then I've been interested in investing and have questioned people who achieved early retirement.

The guy dancing with the redhead reminds me of Sean and something important I learned from him. I remember when Sean seemed to have it all. He had a home with a nice chunk of land east of Springfield and a new four-wheel-drive truck. His wife drove a four-wheel-drive SUV. They had an above-ground pool, satellite TV, a motorcycle, and a nice barn he used as his warehouse.

Unfortunately, he wrecked his motorcycle and ended up with leg and head injuries. He was in the wholesale mattress and delivery business. He even had out-of-state customers, but the business was too mentally and physically demanding for him after the accident. He couldn't do it anymore despite his best efforts. He lost everything and ended up renting from me. I was around thirty years old at the time and was there to collect the rent. He said something I've never forgotten: "I wish I could get a check in the mail instead of a bill! A check big enough to pay the electric bill would be great. Heck, even a check big enough to treat the wife and kid to McDonalds, a check, something, anything!"

I learned an important lesson from Sean, and I didn't even know what it was called then. I did know rental properties were no free lunch. It was earned money that required time as well as reasonably good physical health and mental judgment. A couple of rental houses or a duplex was something of a profitable hobby. Then I bought a couple more houses, and the next thing I knew, all my weekends, holidays and vacations were spent maintaining my properties and collecting rent. This took away from quality time with my family and friends.

I realized he had put most all his investment money in his mattress business, just as I was doing with my rental properties. I was aware of the investment rule, which says to not have all your eggs in one basket (*diversification*), and that was why I felt safer with four houses than a four-unit apartment building, like the one my forty-year-old sailing buddy owned. If there was a fire in one of the four houses, I would lose income from one unit but still have income from the remaining three. If there was a bad fire in his four-unit apartment building, he would lose income on all four.

I realized I needed to diversify further and have unearned income in addition to my earned rental property income. Rather than buy additional rental properties, I needed to find alternative-income streams and let the money flow in month after month, like a never-ending stream, but where could I find a never-ending stream of unearned income? That was the question.

Ever since then, I've been searching for unearned-income streams. What about these widgets? Do they provide a never-ending stream of unearned income, or do they require time and work in order to get fifty cents per month? Unearned income is more valuable to me, because even when I'm home sick, snowed in, banged up, or unable to work, it still comes in. I don't lose my investment, because I'm not there to take care of it.

It looks like the band is getting ready to take a break. I'm ready for one too, because it will give me a chance to visit and find out more about the widgets.

Chapter 3

THE BREAK

The bandleader says he wants to introduce the world-famous Ronald McDonald who has important information on the widgets.

"Hello everyone," he says. He does a balloon trick and then shows us a box labeled "Magic Money Machine." The widgets in the box are like those that will be offered tonight in auction. We are having a contest to see who can best describe what these widgets do, how they work, and what they look like.

Marge, the master of ceremonies, says, "You now know they fit in this box and that they each produce fifty cents per month. What are they? What will you bid? Thanks everyone, and thanks Ronald McDonald! Let's give him a big hand."

There's Bob, a former coworker and school teacher. He earned a major in history and a minor in education. He is smart and has always been able to work amazingly long hours.

I remember when Bob was considering purchasing rental properties and asked me how I did it. I told him my dad was a real estate broker, and I had a real estate license. I had been around real estate my entire life. I managed real estate on a part-time basis, didn't buy anything I wouldn't want to live in, and used only fixed-interest mortgage loans. I went back to school and took real estate law and property management classes at the local community college. Why learn everything from the school of hard knocks? I kept my properties in good repair so that they attracted and retained good tenants and were ready for resale should the need arise. I told him I was careful to keep track of receipts, and I always used the same accountant. I always spent a few minutes talking with him about my return and any tax law changes before signing it.

Some people prepare tax returns for a living, and some people review tax returns for a living. Working together, they are able to correct mistakes before they grow and get out of hand. I told him about being at an IRS foreclosure where IRS guys wore black SWAT uniforms and helmets. I spoke with the people standing in front of the building as we watched the IRS haul away the office furniture, shop tools, equipment, and machines. The workers came to work just like it was any other day, and the next thing they knew, the IRS wanted all the cash and started carrying everything off, including the safe! One worker said, "Guess none of us can expect any more paychecks from here!"

I told Bob the Bible teaches that fear of the Lord is the beginning of wisdom, and I suggested that fear of the IRS is the beginning of financial wisdom. Bob took a different path, and the last I heard, he had 151 houses. He went to auctions, bought property cheap, fixed them up cheap, and rented them. I understood that you couldn't go anywhere without him wanting to make a quick stop to collect rent. It was how he spent all his time. There was a write-up about him in the newspaper, and it more or less called him a "slum lord," showing pictures of his properties that were behind on maintenance.

Someone at the IRS must have read the article and decided to audit him. Rumor had it that the IRS was saying he owed over $250,000 in back taxes and stood to lose most everything. He tried to sell some of his houses to pay the taxes, but the IRS just raised the amount he owed! I'm sure Bob did his best to fill out the tax forms correctly and on time. I remember him saying he took two days off and stayed up most of the night in order to get his tax return completed and in the mail on time. He hired an attorney, and the negotiations are ongoing.

He's looking successful this evening. Earlier, I noticed his new, expensive foreign car. Reliable sources inform me he has been pulling in a healthy six figures.

I say, "Hi, Bob, how are you?"

"Oh, you know how it is," he says. "It's always something. I suppose you heard they had a layoff over at the mill." "Yes, I did hear that. I think it is the first layoff in twenty to thirty years."

"That's right. It's not great paying but steady work. They are usually on time with their rent. That's why I like to rent to them. Now I have half a dozen tenants telling me they can't pay rent. You were a landlord, so you know how it is. The banks want their money every month, and every month you're hoping to collect enough rent to keep the banks off your back. The tenants get drunk, fight, break something, and want you to come and fix it. If it's not fixed within twenty-four hours, they are calling the newspaper."

"That sounds familiar. No doubt about it, rental property is no free lunch. I had that happen to me once. I had a good tenant whose coworker wondered if I had anything available. I did, and things were fine until they both got laid off and couldn't pay their rent. After that I made sure that none of my tenants worked at the same place. You know, not having all your eggs in one basket."

"Good idea. I'm going to remember that. I heard that your wife was in the hospital, and you decided to sell your rental properties."

"Yes, she was in the hospital for weeks and more or less bedridden for months. With teenagers at home, a full-time job, laundry, shopping, and housework, I had enough to do." I decided to bring up the subject we were both interested in: widgets!

"What do you know about the widgets?"

"I doubt I know much more than you, but I think it's for real. I thought it might be some kind of fundraising gag, but I don't think so now."

"Why is that?" I asked.

"I heard from a reliable source that they expect to raise a lot of money tonight. Look at some of the people here. If the widgets are paying six dollars per year each, and we pay one hundred dollars per widget, we earn 6 percent interest [$6 / 100 = .06 or 6 percent] and, according to the *Rule of 72* [72 / interest rate = number of years for money to double], double our money in twelve years [72 / 6 = 12]."

"That's what I come up with too. I suppose it could go up to $120 per widget, but then we would be getting a 5 percent yield [$6 / $120 = .05 or 5 percent], and it would take over fourteen years to double our money [72 / 5 = 14.4]. If we are able to buy widgets tonight for eighty dollars, we would be getting a 7.5 percent return [$6 / $80 = .075], and we would double our money in a little less than ten years [72 / 7.5 = 9.6]."

"My big question is how the income will be taxed." said Bob.

"That is a good question."

It was good seeing and talking to Bob, and he does have a good question. How will the money be taxed? The tax status of the widget is an important factor. There's a big difference between getting the whole six dollars or getting what is left over after federal and state taxes. Usually the federal government wants at least 15 percent, and the state takes a flat 5 percent. If you figure a 20 percent tax rate on six dollars [$6 x .20 = $1.20], you are losing $1.20 to taxes, leaving only $4.80 [$6 - $1.20 = $4.80] to spend or reinvest. Bob has also reminded me how useful the Rule of 72 can be in evaluating both investments and debt.

There's a sight for sore eyes, Jim; he was a member of our clerical support staff over at the old salt mine. We sat near each other for years before I was promoted to Central Office in the Bureau of Financial Policy Research and Analysis. I haven't seen him for years, and since I coached him on personal finances, I am especially eager to see how he's been doing. I think I'll go say hello.

Chapter 4

TABLE TALK

When I approach, I am surprised to hear Jim use the term *tipping point*. I listen as he said, "Bruce, you have reached your financial tipping point when you have enough unearned income (in interest and dividends) to cover basic necessities each month. Think milk, bread, eggs, macaroni, cheese, beans, and rice rather than chips, soda, steak, and beer. Think rabbit ears instead of cable TV. Figure out the least amount of money you need, in case of a financial emergency, to stay in your home, keep your car from being towed, keep food in your refrigerator, and keep the lights, water, and heat on. You can buy a bigger house, car, boat, motorcycle, expensive jewelry, and foreign vacations after you've hit your tipping point! First things first," he says.

I think, "Well put, Jim. If Bruce is smart, he will listen to Jim—he knows what he is talking about."

Jim was one of the most good-hearted and generous men I ever worked with. I remember when he offered a co-worker on renal dialyses a kidney. He was a basketball star in high school, went to war, came home, and Joy was waiting for him. They were high school sweethearts and still liked to go out and dance. In many ways, Jim was the average American guy. He went to work and his paycheck was direct deposited into their joint checking account. He received an allowance to spend, and she took care of the rest. Joy paid their bills, and if they needed something like a new vehicle, she saved for a down payment. They were happy and enjoyed life. Jim was a sports fan and kept up with basketball and baseball, especially his grandsons' baseball careers.

Joy wasn't feeling well for a couple of months, missed work, and had to go on medication. I think it was a wake-up call for both Jim and Joy. His knees had been bothering him as well. I think this happens all the time, especially for people who do "real work." People realize they aren't getting any younger and haven't prepared for retirement. They know what it is to work in pain or when they're not feeling well. They realize that one or both spouses might want or need to retire a year or two sooner than they expected. Medication wasn't free, so Joy needed to reduce Jim's modest allowance, and she had to cut back too.

For the first time, Jim was upset that Joy was controlling all the money. Joy was anxious, because they weren't saving any money, and Jim was unhappy, because he didn't have enough spending money. Jim felt that Joy didn't seem to understand. She got to do all the girl things with their daughters Jill and Jamie. Now it is his chance to do all the boy things with their grandsons. If the boys needed batting practice, he wanted some quarters so they could bat.

If they were hungry, he wanted to be able to buy them a hotdog. Her cutting his allowance could hurt the kid's chances of a college scholarship or even the big leagues. In other words, the situation crossed the line of what was acceptable. He didn't feel like he was getting any respect. After all, he went to work every day, and the Social Security and pension contributions were deducted from his paycheck. A lot of guys were out of work. She should have been grateful instead of treating him like some bum who didn't hold down a job!

Because we were scheduled to get a pay raise after the first of the year, I suggested that Jim put his raise in a savings account at our employee credit union—that way neither he nor Joy would miss it. It could be deducted from his paycheck and automatically deposited just like the Social Security and pension contributions. If he ever felt he needed twenty dollars, he could go down to the second floor and withdraw it from the account. He didn't think Joy would go for that and wasn't into keeping secrets from her. I explained I was not suggesting anything secret. He understood that but knew Joy wouldn't go along with it, and the only way to do it would be to keep it a secret. He didn't see how he could do that, because Joy found out about everything, and he would be in trouble. I told Jim that I understood, and he probably had until December 15 to turn in his payroll deduction authorization to the personnel office, so he had a couple of months to think about it. A couple of weeks before Christmas was the perfect deadline to open a savings account. Jim mentioned he wanted to get some sports equipment for the boys, and the Christmas allowance Joy had allotted him was not enough.

He heard the following commercial on the radio: "Are you short of Christmas money? You don't have to be next year, because you can open a Christmas savings account with us today!" The light bulb clicked on. He remembered what I had suggested but couldn't decide what to do. After hearing the radio commercial, he was ready to turn in his papers, and because it was for Christmas, he didn't feel guilty about keeping it a secret. The raise was deducted from his paycheck, and it went directly into his credit union savings account (this is called *paying yourself first*).

The following year was another tight Christmas, and Joy had some money put aside so that Jim could buy presents. As was the tradition, Joy and the girls took care of the majority of the Christmas shopping. Jim mentioned that Joy seemed suspicious when the boys received all their sports equipment but didn't say anything.

Jim had used our work address for the credit union statements, and it was over a year before it was caught by someone in personnel and the statement was rerouted to his home. At our employee summer picnic, Joy described to me how she went home for lunch and opened it.

At first, she felt betrayed and angry. She thought it was no wonder Jim had extra money, believing he had borrowed money and spent it all on Christmas. Didn't he understand how she'd been pinching pennies and doing without? Now she had one more bill to pay. As she looked at it through angry tears, it slowly dawned on her that it didn't look like a bill. It wasn't a credit card statement! It was a credit union account statement, and Jim had all that money in a credit union account. She was stunned! In a crisis situation like this what was her first instinct? What did she do? She called her daughters, of course, and while she was waiting for them to arrive, called her office and tells them that she had an "emergency" and wouldn't be back that day. Her daughters were there within ten minutes. You can only imagine what happened next.

Chapter 5

THE HOT SEAT

Jim knew Joy would be upset when she found out about his secret savings account and hadn't been looking forward to it. I sat near Jim at work and was there when the phone rang. It was one of his daughters. So from the time Joy called the girls, it was approximately twelve minutes before Jim was on the hot seat. He'd told me in the past how tight Joy and the girls were. The vote was always three to one and he lost!

I heard him say, "Yes, I have an account at the credit union. Why do you ask? Oh, a statement arrived there?" Jim's face was flushed. This was it, the moment of truth, had arrived. "It's my Christmas savings account."

I saw Jim lean back, relax, and he gave me a thumbs up. Everything is turning out better than he dared dream. First off, the "prosecuting attorney" on the phone was not Joy, as he had assumed it would be, and secondly, he could tell by his daughter's tone and choice of words she had already determined that no felony had occurred. Although questioning would continue, it was going to be OK. It didn't happen often, when his daughters came to his defense, but when it did, it was glorious. He couldn't have asked for a better team of defense attorneys. His daughter Jamie had said it was *only* his Christmas savings account but then asked where he got the money.

He said, "Do you remember this Christmas? I wanted to buy the boys their sports equipment last Christmas, but we didn't have the money. I heard a radio ad that said, 'Short on money for Christmas? Don't let it happen again next year, open a Christmas savings account.'" Jim said, [he had this line planned well in advance] "After I heard that commercial, I realized that it's my 'right' as a grandfather to buy my family gifts with my own money."

"It's his 'right' to buy the former prosecuting attorney, now defense attorney, and her son gifts." I thought, "Jim, you are the man!"

He heard Jamie say to her mother and Jill, "Dad says it's his right as a grandfather to buy gifts for his family with his own money. Mother, it doesn't make sense for a working man to have to get money from his wife, so he can buy her a birthday present or Christmas gift. He wants to do it with his own money. What's wrong with that?"

I heard Jim say, "I didn't have any money, and I didn't take the money from anywhere. That's why I went with the PYF program—pay yourself first. I could sign up without any money, but my raise would go into the Christmas savings account. I have been waiting for the statement to see how much is in there. The personal finance coach said that after I got the statement, your mom and I could look at it and see if there was enough money left over from Christmas to pay off one of our charge cards. If there was enough, we could pay it off, go out, celebrate, and cut up the card. Your mother would have one less bill to pay, I could get my allowance back, and I could afford to buy the boys a Coke or hot dog if I want to. I call this the *T play* based on the tipping point. I've realized that we have to start thinking ahead. As the boys grow up, they will have away games, especially after they get scholarships and are playing in college. We'll need extra gas, food, and motel money. The boys just need to remember to keep their grades up."

Jamie now had a clearer picture of the situation. She knew her dad didn't give a hoot what her mom spent or how many charge cards she had as long as she was happy, and he got his allowance. He never discouraged her from buying a dress or shoes or anything else. If anything, Mom was the saver in the family, and Dad was the spender. It was their dad's dream comes true when she and Jill had their boys, less than a year apart. The boys support their grandpa, their biggest fan, on the allowance issue.

She also knew her dad had big plans for the boys, and nothing could stop them, except they had to keep their grades up, or they wouldn't be able to play. Her dad had to sit out a game once, but only once, and according to him, for something not even important; he had received an F in poetry. To hear her dad, grades are the only thing that could keep them from the big leagues. She and Jill both agreed, the boys were lucky to have him.

She also knew her mother. When Dad came back from the war, he got on at the heavy equipment factory, making bulldozers, excavators, and front-end loaders. The husbands of her mom's friends worked at the plant too. They were union jobs and, when they were on overtime, made big money. Because the men were working day and night, the women did the shopping and bill paying. Credit cards were a status symbol in those days. Her mom probably had a dozen cards, and the allowance business started when the plant closed. Her mom went back to work, and they refinanced the house to lower the monthly payment. She got a job in a billing department where she knew people, but even with both parents working, they were making less than when her dad worked at the plant. Her mom said, "The plant raised our girls and took care of our family for twenty-two years."

Her mom made sure she and Jill knew how important it was to have an *emergency fund* that covered six months' worth of bills. She also explained that in order to keep your credit score high, you should never be late with your payments and always pay more than the minimum monthly amount due on your charge cards. Mom shared with them the guidelines she had received from the bank on achieving and keeping a high credit score. Her mother had said that she paid close attention to the bank's suggestions and that was why she was able to have a high credit score and so many charge cards.

The boys asked their grandpa once why grandma paid all the bills, and he got an allowance. He told them,

"Grandma took bookkeeping in high school and got an A, and I took welding and got an A, so if there is any welding to be done, I do it, and if there is any bookkeeping to be done, Grandma does it." He also said, "A lot of families lost their homes when the plant closed, but we didn't. We were lucky your grandma had an emergency fund; otherwise, we would have lost our house too." It's always been that way; Mom has handled the finances ever since Dad went into the service. He sent Mom his marine pay every month, so they could get married when he got home.

Jamie said, "Dad, just to be clear, you talked to a personal financial coach at your work, and you've been waiting for the Christmas fund statement that came today and are wondering if there is enough to pay off a charge card, so Mom won't have to pay that bill, and you can get your allowance back?"

"Yes."

"And if there is enough money, you want to take us out to the family buffet and celebrate by cutting up a charge card? You are also going to pay for it with the money you didn't need from Christmas?

"Yes!"

Jamie turned to her sister, Jill, for assistance. "Jill, remember the people at the hospital who offered a program about savings, charge cards, and retirement?"

"Yes," Jill said.

"Dad talked to one of them at his work, because he wants his allowance back. He wants to do like Trish and Kelli. Are you free for family buffet tonight?"

"Yes," she said. They hadn't gone out to the buffet as a family since Dad's allowance was cut.

Jamie asked, "Can you help Mom pick out a charge card and tell her about Trish and Kelli at the hospital?"

Jill nodded yes and said, "Mom, we had this program at the hospital about charge cards. Some of them charge 18 percent interest! We found out Trish had over $30,000 and Kelli over $36,000 in credit card debt. Trish was paying out over $5,000 dollars per year in interest, and Kelli was paying over $6,000. Can you believe that?"

Jill told me at the summer picnic how her mother had been sitting there stiff, enduring, and looking straight ahead as if her world was falling apart. When Jill mentioned Trish and Kelli, she sighed, and her shoulders dropped. It was as if she had been carrying all the financial responsibilities ever since the war and felt like a failure in her daughters' eyes.

Jill said, "We looked at each other and understood. Our father's plant closed about the time we were getting ready to graduate from high school. Our mom had told us it was a good thing Dad had gotten a job before his unemployment ran out, or we probably would have lost the house like so many others. Jamie and I were both accepted into a work program that paid almost all our tuition for nursing school, but we both knew that Mom had used charge cards to pay for our books and supplies. If she had $30,000 in charge card debt, at least $20,000 of it had been spent on us."

Jill gently said, "Mom, can I help you find an ugly old credit card that Dad can pay off and cut up, so we can all go out tonight and celebrate him getting his allowance back?"

Still in a state of shock, she nodded and said in almost a whisper, "Yes, and he can leave $200 in there."

Jamie said, "Dad, Mom has a charge card you can pay off and cut up, so we can all go out tonight and celebrate you getting your allowance back. She also says you can leave $200 in your Christmas account."

Jamie then said in a low voice, with her hand covering the mouth piece of the phone, "Dad, you know Mom hasn't got to go to the river boat with her friends since you guys started pinching pennies and your allowance was cut. Since you're getting your allowance back, and I know Jill will agree with me on this, I think you should not leave that $200 in there but give it to Mom, so she can go play blackjack with her friends. It's only once a year, and she doesn't spend any more money than you do to attend a big league ball game. When you pay off another card this time next year, you might get another increase in your allowance. Maybe for every charge card you pay off for Mom, she can give you another allowance increase."

I saw Jim put his left hand up in the air, clinch it into a fist, and pull it down, saying, "Yessssss!"

Jim was on cloud nine. He had dreaded the day Joy would find out about the account, but things could not have gone more perfectly. He was going to have money for presents and equipment the boys needed, and he was getting his allowance back. He hadn't thought about a buffet with the entire family to celebrate, but that was icing on the cake. He didn't like feeling less in front of the boys, like he did when his allowance was cut and just as Joy did when the girls realized she had credit card debt.

It was after Jamie and Jim got off the phone that Joy and the girls talked about finances. The family had never discussed the subject except for the emergency fund and good credit scores. Jim and Joy had an emergency fund from the first day of their marriage. Joy explained how their family income dropped when the plant closed and how she used the emergency money to pay the mortgage and other bills. She explained that even after returning to work, she had not been able to put any money into the emergency fund. She had been taught that you needed to have a "rainy day fund," and it bothered her to not have one, especially when she was not feeling well and had missed some work. Her fear was that without an emergency fund, if something bad happened, they could lose the house. She thought that by pinching pennies and cutting their dad's allowance, she could keep up with all the payments until the house was paid off. When there was no house payment, she could build up the emergency fund and pay off the credit cards.

Joy had been so focused on not losing the house and building up the emergency fund that the only thing she had worried about was paying more than the minimum on the charge cards and keeping her credit scores high. So, if anything was needed (such as the girls' nursing school books and supplies), they had the money.

THE HOT SEAT

The girls pointed out that Joy owed $24,000 on her charge cards. Jill said, "Mom, it looks like you are paying about $3,600 per year in interest. The finance people from our credit union said they can give half-price loans to pay off credit cards. That's what Trish and Kelli did. It would save you about $1,800 per year in interest. That's $150 per month you could put in your emergency fund. As we say at the hospital, you can't know what no one has ever told you." Jill still had the workbook she had received from the finance program at work. She said, "I'll make a quick run to the hospital and get it. You might as well look at the pictures in the workbook rather than have Dad try to draw them for you."

Joy and the girls knew how it was when he started drawing sports plays on paper.

Jill returned with the workbook and said, "Mom, Trish is on duty today, and I spoke with her. She says just go with the flow and don't worry. These personal finance coaches practically brainwash the men on charge cards and build it up as if it was a mortgage burning. The whole family gets to go eat out and celebrate when one gets cut up, so save them. Pay off one whenever we all need to celebrate."

Joy liked the idea of having extra money each month for the emergency fund. Her financial "aircraft" would no longer be at risk of crashing. Burning the house mortgage would be like a safe landing after flying through a storm. Her biggest financial concern throughout the plant closing storm had been losing their home. She and her mother found it while Jim was still serving overseas. Her mother said it was big enough to raise a family in but not too big once the kids moved out. She looked forward to not having a mortgage payment, and it would be a relief to not worry about losing the house. It had been an emotional roller coaster ride, but with Jim paying off the charge cards, she didn't feel like they were on a sinking ship anymore.

She was glad Jill still had her workbook, and it was helpful. She decided to spruce up and pick out a nice dress. She picked out a card to cut up: one of the cards she had used to help the girls with nursing school. She understood what Jill was talking about. Cutting a charge card in two was like a celebration of "burning the mortgage."

She thought, "Not exactly a romantic evening, but having the whole family at the buffet will be fun. If I understand the workbook correctly, Jim is supposed to pay for the evening in cash. This will be interesting."

She felt better and wondered if her worry over finances had anything to do with her headaches and high blood pressure.

Chapter 6

FEAR

Jim was in good spirits as he went on his afternoon break. He went downstairs to the credit union and withdrew all but the fifty dollars needed to keep the account open. He had six fifty-dollar bills and a cashier's check when he got back from break. He hadn't had more than fifty dollars in his hands for years and was a nervous wreck. He was surprised there was so much money in the Christmas account. He acted like it was a hot potato. He couldn't wait to hand it off to Joy but wasn't looking forward to facing her. We had a plan.

Joy needed to cut one of her cards in two and give him half. She could keep half, and Jim would give her a cashier's check to pay off the charge card and $150 cash for the river boat. Jim knew he could trust Joy to pay off the charge card. The rest of the money, $150, was for him to pay for the family buffet that night. Any money leftover could go in his coffee can in the garage, or he could give it to Joy for the emergency fund.

Jim told me he liked the idea of an extra twenty dollars' worth of quarters in reserve. He told me quarters worked out the best with his grandsons. The wind didn't blow them, and if something cost seventy-five cents, he could give them each three quarters.

I said, "Okay, I understand, but at some point, remind Joy the $150 is for the boat with her friends, not the emergency fund. It is best for her to cut the card in two and give you half but help her if she needs it. You don't have to wait to give her the check and boat money at the restaurant. She can cut the card in two there at the house and give you your "trophy" as a reminder that your allowance is restored. Once you have your trophy, your mission has been accomplished. She may want to put her cash in a safe place and deposit the check on the way to the buffet. This is a celebration. Hopefully, you can do this again. It's one payment you don't have to make every month. Think tipping point!"

Jim said he was nervous on the way home. He put the cash in his wallet and the check in his coat pocket. He worried about the car breaking down or somehow losing the money before he could get it to Joy. It was probably a good thing. If he thought that Joy was angry with him he, like most men, would lay low and wait for things to cool down. Because he was more afraid of losing the money than facing Joy, he was going to get the hard part done right away.

Jim told me about a time when he had to take ammo up to a machine gun. He was carrying over one hundred pounds of machine gun belts, he stumbled, and, for no reason, he believed an angel pushed him. He fell just as he heard and felt the wind of a bullet pass within an inch of his ear. He was lying there on the ground, miraculously alive, and the enemy was shooting at him. "They were trying to kill me, and I was too scared to move! Did my buddies come out from behind the sandbags to help me carry that ammo? No! They hollered, 'Crawl Jim, crawl!' When I was finally able to move, I started crawling and got over the sandbags."

The safest place to be, according to Jim, when you were out on patrol was in the center of the squad—not rear guard or point but in the middle. That's where the radioman always was, because communication was critical. One day, Jim's squad was out on patrol, and a bolt of lightning hit the radioman's antenna. The corpsman said there was nothing he could do, and the radioman was killed instantly. The bullet missing him and the bolt of lightning hitting the radioman proved to Jim that if the Good Lord decided it was your time, it was your time!

I tell this story for two reasons. First, I believe his experience in war taught him not to worry too much about planning ahead, and second, Jim told me he would have probably ended up like other combat veterans with shell shock (also known as Post Traumatic Stress Disorder or PTSD) if it hadn't been for Joy and his dad. When he came home, there was the couch in the living room, just like he remembered it, and he was exhausted. He just wanted to sleep. He was back in the old neighborhood, and no one was trying to kill him. His dad was awake and on guard. He said he slept on the couch for a couple of days, and his dad decided it was enough of that. He said, "The plant's hiring, you're getting married, and you will have a family to support. Get up and get your application in."

Jim started working the next Monday. He didn't even get a two-week vacation and was irritated with his dad at the time, but when he saw what happened to many others, he knew that his dad was right. He had both his eyes, hands, and feet, so he was lucky. He didn't get a "Dear John" letter like so many other guys.

Joy and her mother had looked at houses and had a plan to buy one. It needed some work but was in a good neighborhood. Jim and Joy could rent it until he worked at the plant long enough to qualify for a loan. Once the loan went through, and it was theirs, Joy had the money saved to pay for the repairs. Jim had always known that he had a jewel in Joy. He never wanted to fight with her—he had enough fighting to last a lifetime. He told me more than once he could easily have been like the homeless veterans if it hadn't been for his dad and Joy. He gave his dad and Joy the credit for basically saving his life. He was about to rediscover how much of a jewel he really had.

Chapter 7

FACE TO FACE

Jim took a deep breath as he grabbed the door handle and went in. Joy was standing in the kitchen, as beautiful as ever.

He hated this part, but he knew he needed to complete his mission. Otherwise everything would be ruined, and the tipping point play wouldn't work. He said, "I've got the check here to pay off a charge card. It proves that the personal finance coach's tipping point play works. We've got to pay off the credit cards one by one and cut them in two. They are charging us 15 percent on average. You can buy a new car for 2.9 percent, so at 15 percent, we're paying double or more for everything. I learned about the Rule of 72."

Joy replied, "I learned about the rule too."

"You did?"

"Yes. After you got off the phone, the girls explained that they had a program at their work and knew what you were talking about. Jill brought her book over for me. Some of the words you were using are in here. Here is a picture of the tipping point. If we are going to follow the book, it's time to cut up a credit card."

The card was lying on the counter, and she pulled a knife out of the butcher block. She said, "Do you have the check for me?"

"Yes, and I can do that." He never liked watching her work with a large knife. She had such beautiful hands, and he didn't like the idea of her cutting herself.

"You are supposed to get half, and I'm supposed to get half, correct?"

"Yes."

He took his half of the credit card and gave her the check. She looked at it and said, "Jim, I want you to know this check is paying the charge card I used to buy the girls' nurses uniforms for graduation and some of their books." She gave him a quick hug, said thank you, and suggested they deposit the check on the way to the buffet.

Jim had his trophy but was confused. He had received a quick hug and thank you, but it was obvious to him he wasn't completely out of the doghouse for the secret that caused her to be upset. Joy seemed to understand everything he was trying to explain. The workbook was a surprise but a good one, and everything was going so well he almost forgot he had Joy's boat money in his wallet.

Joy could see this wasn't easy for him. She recognized Jim's body language and saw the same gestures he has used with the boys when he was pleading with them to keep their grades up. She had learned a lot by reading Jill's personal finance workbook. She liked the idea of refinancing the charge cards at the credit union. The credit union's interest rate was half of what her charge cards were. She could understand why Jim felt that getting rid of the charge cards was just as important as the boys keeping their grades up.

This was a big check, and she will be glad to have it deposited.

They went to the drive-up window and sent the check through the tube. When she had the receipt in her hand, she looked at it as they left the bank. She still could not believe Jim had saved all that money, and, as they drove to the buffet, the ramifications were sinking in. It wasn't just one less payment. It was hope for the future, and she was surprised at how nice it felt. She was starting to feel hungry and realized she had forgotten to eat lunch. Yes, she had been upset.

They arrived at the buffet, and their daughters and grandsons were there waiting. Jim said it was great they could get together on such short notice, and it was too bad the boy's dads couldn't make it. The hours the girls worked were always changing. Hospitals are open twenty-four hours a day, seven days a week, so they and their husbands juggled their work schedules to take care of everything.

Usually Jim was talking to his sons-in-law and the boys as they entered the buffet and Joy paid. Joy was prepared to pay, but she held back. Jim said it felt good to pull out those two fifty-dollar bills and pay with cash. Because his sons-in-law hadn't been able to make it, the total with tax and tip was under one hundred dollars, leaving Jim with twenty dollars, a pound of quarters for his coffee can, and an extra fifty-dollar bill. Jim could tell that the girls approved and were happy not to be cooking. The boys were happy, because the buffet was one of their favorite places, right up there with McDonalds!

Joy was still putting on her public face, and Jim had a plan coming together once everyone went through the food line and was seated. He moved the $150 boat money from his wallet to his shirt pocket and decided it was the perfect time to seal the deal on his allowance. He said to the boys, "We're celebrating three things tonight. Your grandma and I paid off your moms' nursing school, which means I get my allowance back. Your mothers and I agree that if I am getting my allowance back, your grandma should get to go to the riverboat with her friends!"

Jim took three fifty-dollar bills out of his pocket and handed them to Joy. She was surprised and happy! She gave Jim a hug and a kiss on the cheek as the girls and the boys applauded. Jim told her the personal finance coach said to remind her that the money was for the boat, not the emergency fund.

At that moment, her emergency fund was the last thing on her mind. "No problem," she thought. "This personal finance coach does seem to know what he's doing."

Jim had planned to tell Jill and Jamie he had to keep fifty dollars in the account to keep it open, and he could see the way they were looking at him; he was fifty dollars short. Since the boys' dads couldn't make it, he had extra money in his wallet. He said, "The personal finance coach said that your mother is 100 percent right about the emergency fund and she will enjoy her outing even more knowing that the fifty dollars in my wallet are going into the emergency fund."

Now the girls were even thinking, "This personal finance coach is pretty good. They can live with it, and besides, what can you do? It's like an umpire call.

Joy told Jim it was at this point she actually felt joyful. He thought her eyes looked moist. She took Jim's hand in hers and held it tight. They both ate with one hand and Jim understood being solely responsible for their finances had been stressful for her. The personal finance coach was right. Taking care of all the finances and paying the bills was a big responsibility, and since the plant closed, he hardly ever welded anymore.

"The personal finance coach said something else too. You haven't been to the boat for a while, so there's a chance you may have a lucky winning streak. He suggested you stop gambling once you have enough winnings to pay off a charge card. Every month you don't make the payment is like you're adding to your winnings. Instead of just winning $500, you end up with $1,000 or more! The coach said the earlier in the day you have your winning streak, the harder it is to quit. The natural tendency is to keep going while you're on a hot streak and go home without any money, but if you quit while you're ahead, you come home a winner, we pay off a bill, we all get to come here again, and you already have money to go back to the boat with your friends again next year!"

They all agreed that it was hard to argue with the math. They would come home winners more often if they knew "when to fold them" as the country song goes.

Jim didn't come into work the next day. He and Joy had decided to spend the day together resting. Jim said Joy cried when they got home and told him it felt like he was finally back from the war. She showed him all the charge card bills and what they had each purchased. None of the money was wasted. She also showed him their emergency account balance of less than one month's worth of expenses.

He told me he read Jill's personal finance workbook, and emergency fund was listed. He was glad they knew enough to have an emergency fund, and he wished he had known about the tipping point, paying yourself first, the Rule of 72, and unearned income when he was making big money at the plant. Life would have been much easier if he and Joy had known this stuff. He realized some of their cards charged 18 percent interest. According to the Rule of 72, seventy-two divided by eighteen equals four, which meant that at 18 percent interest, they doubled their money every four years. Therefore, if he and Joy paid off a charge card they would in effect be earning 18 percent on their money. Where else could they earn 18 percent on their money?

Jim had learned that often the best investment a person can make is debt reduction. In fact, even if you have high-interest debt, such as charge cards, paid off, you can pay off your mortgage early as Kathy Kristof wrote in the *Kiplinger's Personal Finance Magazine.* "A home can be an effective savings plan for those of us who pay a little extra toward the mortgage each month."[1] Twenty years later, she reaped a "huge" reward!

1 Kathy Kristof, "History Says Stick With Stocks" *Kiplinger's Personal Finance* August 2013, 42

Chapter 8

BACK AT THE TABLE

I haven't seen Jim in years and say, "It's good to see you. I heard you explaining the tipping point, nicely done."

"Thanks Coach, and it is good to see you too. It was one of the most important things I ever learned. I wish I would have learned about it much sooner. Speaking of much sooner, I'll bet that soccer player from Africa wished he had known something about personal finance much sooner. Did you hear about that?"

"No, I haven't."

"He was some kid from a small village who could run fast and had a gift for soccer. He had never had any money before but ended up a famous big league soccer player, making three million dollars per year. He had a career-ending injury around year five and had made about fifteen million dollars. His injury happened two years ago, and today, he is broke! Can you believe that? He made fifteen million dollars, and two years later, he says he can't afford a pair of tennis shoes. He's broke, barefoot, and back in the village where he started. If he had a great personal finance coach like you, he would still have all that money and probably a lot more."

"Thanks Jim. I appreciate it. Believe it or not, stories like that are not unusual. Some people win the lotto and are broke a year or two later. Think of the music, acting, and sport stars who are on top for a year or two and then are right back where they started."

"When the boys make the big leagues, I'll tell them to look you up."

"That would be quite a feather in my cap. How are their sports careers going?" I asked.

"They are both playing varsity baseball this year and doing great."

"How have you and Joy been doing?"

"Real well; once we had the charge cards paid off, we were able to build up the emergency fund. We requested an amortization schedule from our mortgage lender as you had suggested. Looking at the amortization schedule was a real learning experience. It showed all the monthly payments we had made, how much of the payment went to interest, and how much went to reduce the loan balance. I hadn't realized that paying a little extra each month could get the house paid off so much quicker."

I agree, "It is amazing."

Jim said, "If I had been smart and known about the tipping point, I could have had the house paid off before the plant closed. Joy says living in a paid-off house is the best emergency fund or disability insurance there is, and I agree.

We kept paying off charge cards and staying in the groove, just like pitching and throwing strikes. We also kept adding to the emergency fund. Joy watched the balances, and once there was enough in the emergency fund, we paid off the house and had a "mortgage burning party." You were right; becoming debt-free and owning a well-insulated home in good repair is wonderful!"

"I remembered what you said about unearned sources of never-ending streams of income. It made a lot of sense to Joy and me. We're not that many years away from qualifying for Social Security, and any extra income won't hurt anything. I can't wait to find out about these widgets."

"I can't either." I said.

Chapter 9

THE WINNER

Ronald McDonald and Marge call Arlene up to the stage and tell her she won the contest, because she most accurately described the widget. "Arlene, can you read for the audience what you wrote?" Marge says.

"It looks a lot like the change machine at the Laundromat. You put in five dollars, and it gives you twenty quarters."

"Thank you, Arlene. Here is your gift card for twenty dollars, redeemable at your local McDonalds"

Everyone applauds, and Arlene goes to sit down.

Marge says, "Wouldn't that be great to own forty widgets and get eighty quarters per month from now on? Think about it—one whole pound of quarters every month, tax-free, for the rest of your life! You heard me. I said tax-free."

She has my attention. I can only think of one way they could do something like that, and now it all makes perfect sense. She said the widgets were going to be sold in groups of ten tonight. Ten widgets will be the lowest amount of widgets you can buy.

"Ten widgets produce five dollars per month or a quarter-pound of quarters every month—in other words, a never-ending source of tax-free income. Forty widgets produce twenty dollars per month or one pound of quarters. In one year, you would have twelve pounds of quarters to spend any way you want. What if you are off work and at home with no income? A pound of quarters would come in mighty handy, wouldn't it? You could buy gas and go to McDonalds! We will have more information later in the program regarding the widgets. Now back to the music."

This reminds me of something one of my favorite uncles told me. He was in his eighties at the time and said I had better believe twenty dollars was a lot of money in retirement. He worked at the community college, keeping the place up, and he had a modest pension and Social Security. One thing that always amazed me about him was his knowledge of automobiles and trucks. He always seemed to know all the options on new vehicles, and he owned some nice cars and trucks through the years. He said he regretted buying a new vehicle before his old one was paid off. He got good deals. The dealerships gave him a good price on his trade, and the payment didn't go up much, if at all, but instead of the vehicle being paid off in two or three years, it was now five.

He said, "If someone has paid two or three years on a vehicle loan and takes out another five-year loan, what happens? It is simple arithmetic. They will be making payments eight years in a row. What if they do it a second or third time? They are making vehicle payments every month for twenty years. You better believe that adds up to a lot of money. We would have been better off to do like your aunt Martha. She would buy a car new, follow the maintenance schedule, and keep driving it several years after it was paid off. That's the smart way to do it. When you look back over your lifetime, there will be many months you won't have a car payment. Do you know what else she did? She called the phone, electric, and gas companies, spoke with their investor relations departments and told them she was interested in their *dividend reinvestment program* or DRIP. She signed up, and every month she didn't have a car payment, she sent them some money. Now that she's retired the phone, electric and gas companies send her money! Your aunt Martha was thinking with her head!"

My uncle is correct. Can you imagine how much interest you would pay, if you paid interest each month for thirty or forty years? Can you imagine how much interest you could have earned? As my dad explained to me years ago, "I've learned it's better to earn interest than pay interest." Think of all the companies you pay every month. Wouldn't it be nice if you were receiving checks from them? Wouldn't it be especially nice during a cold winter with high heating bills or a hot summer with high cooling bills?

Twenty dollars per month is a lot of money when you're old and can't see well enough to drive. Just imagine receiving one pound of quarters every month from now until you are in your eighties. What would it be like to say, "I bought some widgets a couple of years ago, and I've already received twenty-four pounds of quarters?" How much would it cost to purchase a twenty dollar never-ending stream of tax-free monthly income?

Chapter 10

SMOKE BREAK

Now is a good time to go out for a smoke break and light up my pipe. My granddad smoked a pipe. He was good to us and gave us quarters to go to the ball park, just like Jim did with his grandkids.

My dad told me Granddad said, "It's not what you make; it's what you save!" He didn't trust banks after the Great Depression. He had coffee cans full of quarters under the kitchen sink, in his bedroom, in the shed, and in the garage. As far as I know, this was the only kind of "investing" he did. After Grandma passed away, his main goal was to pay off the hospital bills, because he didn't want to leave debt for his kids. He worked as a barber well into his seventies. It's sad when you stop to think about it. I believe he worked for every dime he ever had. His money never earned him anything. It just sat around in cans gathering dust.

Another pipe smoker was a man in the old neighborhood. His name was Merle, and he retired early. He was an investor, and I asked him if he had any advice. He said, "If a man makes $100 a week and spends ninety, in the long run, it will work out. If a man makes $1,000 a week and spends $1,010, in the long run, that won't work out."

Another person I asked advice from was my accountant, Herb, who was retiring early. He leaned back, thought about it and said, "The best advice I can give you is 'get out of debt, stay out of debt'!"

Here comes Marge. She says, "Hey, Coach, I thought I would find you out here. It's good to see you."

"Marge, you caught me; large crowd tonight."

"Yes, it looks like our dream is coming together, and I wanted to thank you for all your help in answering questions and giving me ideas."

"You're most welcome."

"Do you remember the dairy farm story you told me? I've been thinking about using your story and wanted to make sure you had no objection."

"That is considerate of you, Marge. You're welcome to use the story if you want to."

"Thanks, Coach. I would love to stay outside and chat, but I need to get back to work."

"I understand."

"That was quick," I thought. "This should be interesting." Marge looks busy, tying up a few loose ends.

Paul, my first real stockbroker, also retired early. It was around 1980 after a big increase in the price of gold, and I was interested. I thought, "Do some research and go in to a large stock brokerage firm." I was introduced to John, a young broker, and he felt that it wasn't the best time to invest in precious metals. He told me the firm was *bearish* (meaning the price should go down) on precious metals, especially silver and it looked ready for a tumble. I was introduced to *calls* (betting that a stock will go up in a specified amount of time). I was also introduced to *puts* (betting that prices will go down within a specified amount of time). Eastman Kodak used a lot of silver, and a price drop in silver would be *bullish* (meaning the price should go up), so we bought a call on Eastman Kodak.

I wasn't with this broker very long even though I made some quick money. I realized with his plan of action, time was against me, and not for me! I decided if a stock was cheap, I should buy it. It would probably go up over time, but it seemed unwise to bet that a stock would go up or down within a few months. The stockbroker was fired because he lost some of the company's long-term customers a lot of money. He wasn't acting in my best interest as an investment advisor; he was acting as a bookie. Win or lose, he would earn fees.

My next broker was good old Paul, and he introduced me to income investing. This was in the old days when men would go in to the stockbroker's office, sit on the wood bench, and watch the ticker. I remember one old guy jumping up, saying, "Buy beans, Paul, buy beans" and, twenty minutes later, saying, "Sell beans, Paul, sell beans." He had made $700 and did a little dance for us. "Not bad," I thought.

However, Paul wanted me to know about utility stocks, such as electric, gas, and phone companies. These were companies that would send me a dividend check every three months for the rest of my life. Once I owned some shares, I could enroll in a DRIP (dividend reinvestment program). Every three months, instead of the company sending me a check, the money would be used to purchase more stock. The amount I received would grow, because every three months, I would have more shares that produced more income. I could also mail checks directly to the company to purchase more stock without having to pay a brokerage commission, and I could stop reinvesting at any time. The companies would resume mailing me the quarterly checks instead of reinvesting them.

"Remember," Paul said, "the longer you let the dividends snowball [compound]," "the bigger the checks will be when you start drawing them. It works a lot like a bond fund."

He was right! Unfortunately, he was my broker for less than two years. His firm moved to a larger city about an hour and a half away. He could keep his job and move or retire early. His house was paid off, and neither he nor his wife wanted to move from their family home. They did not want to miss out on any opportunities to babysit their grandchildren. He felt blessed to have his dividend income so he could retire and not move, and he said I was young enough to do the same thing. I was around thirty years old at the time; Paul had five kids and was fifty-three!

The dividend reinvestment programs provided for the reinvestment of dividends and also the direct purchase of shares without a broker's commission, and they worked well for me, Aunt Martha, and Paul. Do you think it would be enjoyable or comforting to find checks in your mailbox instead of bills? I think of utility companies (phone, electric, water, gas, and waste removal) as eternal. Some are over one hundred years old and most likely will be around for another hundred years. My first stream of never-ending unearned income was utility stocks.

I hear Marge calling everyone back inside. She has an announcement and is going to give us some background on the widgets.

Chapter 11

THE DAIRY FARM

Marge says, "Hi everyone. I think most of you know me. I'm the manager of the local Ronald McDonald House. As you all know, we promised you more information, so I thought I would start with a story about a dairy farm as told by a personal financial coach who volunteers at the shelter. I heard him talking about never-ending streams of unearned income, Laundromats, bonds, and dairy farms. I asked him if that was like a bond I had bought for $1,000. I get a dividend twice a year for ten years, and then I get my $1,000 back.

"He said, 'Close, but a bond has a maturity date; it expires.' He said, 'Think of a milk cow and a bond as alike in that neither one is eternal. If you buy a young milk cow, for example, she could give milk for several years before she dries up and you sell her. Buy a bond, and it gives a dividend several years before it matures, and you get your original investment back.'

"I said I read in *Kiplinger's Personal Finance Magazine* that when interest rates go up, bonds go down. This didn't make sense to me, because I bought a bond for $1,000, I receive my dividend payment twice a year, and in ten years, I get my $1,000 back.

"Coach said, 'I think what they are referring to is if a bond is sold before it matures. You could get less for your bond if interest rates go up, and you sell early.'

"I said, 'This reminds me of a bank certificate of deposit. It's almost like I took out a contract on the ten-year bond. If I decide to cash it in before my ten years are up, I could get less for my "pre-owned" bond.'

"Coach said, 'Yes, if interest rates go up, but unlike certificates of deposit, or CDs, if rates go down, you could get more. Think of it this way. If interest rates have risen, that means the shiny new bonds are paying more than your 'pre-owned' bonds. If you want to sell your pre-owned bonds, you need to lower your price, so your current yield, or annual income, divided by the price of the bond, equals that of a new bond. On the other hand, if interest rates are dropping, and the shiny new bonds are yielding less, think of your pre-owned bond as an antique. It is yielding more and is worth more than the shiny new bonds. In your situation, this is all academic, since your plan is to simply collect dividends until the bond matures.'

"I said, 'Coach, what does this have to do with washing machines? I heard you talking about a Laundromat and dairy farms. I also overheard you talking about never-ending streams of income, and I thought you said bonds.'

"He said, 'My washing machine at home broke down, and I'm waiting on a washing machine part, so I recently went to the local Laundromat. I've been meaning to tell you how expensive it is, and if you do decide to provide laundry facilities at Ronald McDonald House, you really need two washing machines and dryers. Residents could do their whites in one machine and darks in another. Once you wash and dry a couple of loads of laundry, you've gone through close to half a pound of quarters! I think you have a great idea for having laundry machines at the shelter. It would not only be more convenient for the residents but surely less expensive.'

"I sent a memo to my supervisor. She thought it was a great idea too, and she sent it to the top! They liked the idea but asked how we were going to pay for the washers and dryers. It was not in the budget, and they didn't want to do anything that would jeopardize our nonprofit status. We had permission to go ahead as long as we could work out the financing and didn't make a profit.

Marge has the audience's rapt attention.

"Isn't this always the problem? Money?" she asked.

Chapter 12

LAID OFF

It surprises me that nearly the entire audience nods in agreement. I look at Bob, and he shrugs. We realize we are in the minority on this issue.

When we worked together, he was full time during the summers and part time during the school year. He was the only coworker I had who was interested in investments. We talked about rental properties and utility stocks. We took turns winning contests and prizes, and we were making more than the company vice president some weeks! I was in my twenties, healthy, and able to work a ton of hours, and so was Bob. We were in the right place at the right time. It was great money for four or five years until it started slowing down, so I recall when money was an issue. I learned some important lessons at a young age.

Our company was being bought out. Less than two months previously, management called our department in for a meeting, and we were told not to worry; everyone's job was secure. Within two weeks of the deal closing, our entire department was called in for a routine meeting, and the new company laid us off! I was a star employee who had been assured of job security and a promotion in an exciting new industry, and suddenly I was out of work! They handed us our six weeks of severance pay. The manager of the old company gave me a great reference, which meant more to me than anything else.

I know the shock and soul searching that goes on when you have unexpectedly lost your first job, or your dream job, for reasons beyond your control and through no fault of your own. In fact, much of personal finance planning has to do with preparing for unexpected loss of income. As they say, life happens!

I didn't feel so cocky walking into the unemployment office, but I did it, even though I was still in shock. I had paid into the program, never believing I would use it. It wasn't that different from what I had experienced in the navy. In those days, unemployment benefits lasted three months. The amount of money was barely enough to buy food and pay the mortgage. Do you think having an emergency fund helped me sleep at night? It did, but not at first. I liked my job and the people I worked with. I had planned to retire from there.

With rental property, I knew about the importance of an emergency fund. I never knew when I would have an unexpected expense or a tenant couldn't pay the rent because of job loss, divorce, or hospitalization.

I learned debt is a two-edged sword. It's great to buy a house with a small down payment when you have a job

you like and are making good money. You can buy several houses, like I did. This is called using *leverage*. For
example, if you had $50,000, you could buy one house, or
you could buy five houses or more. To buy five houses, you
would put $10,000 (or 20 percent) down on each house
and borrow the rest. You would still owe $40,000 on each
and $200,000 total. Say that your house payments were
$400 per month each, for a total of $2,000. You could rent
four of the houses for $500 per month, giving you $2,000.
This would be enough money for you to live in the fifth
one for free.

Why put up with all the hassles of property management
to have a free house to live in when you could pay cash in
the first place and live in a paid-off house without the headaches? There are a couple of reasons. The first is that in
twenty years, the tenants will have paid off all five properties for you. You have $2,000 in monthly income in addition
to a free place to live. To a young man with a good job and
no children, this sounded like a good deal. It didn't sound
nearly as good being unemployed with a wife and baby.

The second reason was that I didn't have $50,000 in cash,
so I saved up and bought one house per year for five years.
On one of my properties, the bank let me put down only 5
percent, or $2,500, because I was moving closer to work and
living in the home. I learned higher leverage meant higher
risk. In other words, the less money I put down on a property, the higher my monthly payment. This was not good,
especially if I was unemployed or the property vacant. Even
if I was employed and it was rented, my profit was less each

month. I needed to have enough profit each month to cover maintenance and vacancy expenses.

I probably lost, on average, one tenant per year. When I lost a tenant, I also generally lost a month's rent. The property often needed to be painted, repaired, and the carpets shampooed. The new tenant usually moved in the first of the next month. Occasionally, I might go a year or two without any turnovers. On average, I lost one or two month's rent per year. This is no big deal if you've got a job, but when you're unemployed, debt is a major stressor. It made me realize the importance of having a well-maintained and paid-off home. One of life's storms can hit you when you least expect it.

Instead of buying the fourth and fifth properties, I wish I had put the money into the house we were living in. I would have done a few important things sooner. My utility bills were high, but I hadn't noticed it when I was working, and I hadn't noticed the single-pane windows and wooden entry doors. I couldn't believe the difference double-pane, energy-efficient windows and insulated doors made in the comfort of our home. Half of the rear door had been a single-pane window! The new exterior doors and double-pane windows lowered our electric bills in the summer and our gas bills in the winter. I added insulation in the attic to help the house stay warm in the winter and put in roof vents to help the house stay cool during the summer. Our utility bills dropped nearly 40 percent! We were saving thirty-five to forty dollars per month or over $400 per year.

The other thing I could have done was refinance the house. Instead of buying two more houses, I could have put $20,000 down on our home, refinanced, and had the payment lowered. When you are unemployed, a house payment of $200 per month sounds a lot better than a $400 payment. I didn't know I could request a copy of my *amortization schedule* from the bank. When I did, it surprised me how little of the $400 went toward the *principal* (the amount owed). It was less than 10 percent of the payment! I was paying $400 per month, and only thirty or forty dollars were going toward what I owed!

Once you get your amortization schedule and loan balance, you see exactly how much the principal is being reduced each month. On one of my properties, it was only twenty-nine dollars. If I added twenty-nine dollars to my payment, it was like making two house payments instead of one! I had been paying on houses for years, but why did it not dawn on me that I could pay these houses off much sooner for so little money? I could have been using compound interest to my advantage. As they said at the hospital, you can't know what no one has ever told you.

Fortunately, I had learned about diversifying my income streams and was doing like my aunt Martha. For the months when all the units were rented, I sent money to utility companies. My utility stocks paid me about $375 every three months, and I reinvested the dividends. I didn't want to sell unless I absolutely had to, but I couldn't afford to reinvest the dividends until I returned to work. I called the utility companies, cancelled the reinvestment, and started receiving the checks in the mail. Do you think $375 helps when you've lost your job? It pays for groceries, utility bills, and gasoline as you look for a new job. If you have three to five utility companies sending you checks every three months, it helps! If you update your home and reduce your utility bills by an average of thirty-five dollars per month, it helps. They both help your tipping point!

I talked to Bob about the layoff and was genuinely surprised. What had been a traumatic event for me wasn't a big a deal for him, because it was his second job. He purchased his first rental house at an auction during the layoff. It was over a year before I was called back to work, and I did receive a promotion. I was happy to have my family insured again. I restarted the dividend reinvestment programs on my utility stocks. If I ever had any doubt about alternative sources of unearned income, they were gone. My accountant's words of wisdom, "get out of debt, stay out of debt," were heard loud and clear.

If I had been hit with a major medical bill or a couple of vacancies, it could have been much worse. I could easily have been Tom. I got laid off just like him and neither one of us had our houses paid off. What if I had been laid off one year sooner? What if I had lost my insurance a year sooner or my daughter been born a year later?

Ronald McDonald House makes me proud that I worked at McDonald's during high school and college. The owner talked to me about becoming a manager after I graduated.

LAID OFF

It would have been a great plan. Other guys have done very well with them over the years. It's funny how the draft and a war can change a man's life but enough daydreaming. I better pay attention to what Marge is saying on the stage.

Chapter 13

COOPERATIVES

Marge says, "We are so grateful for all the volunteers do. We couldn't run the Ronald McDonald House Charities if it wasn't for the volunteers. Everyone is so generous with their donations and time that I knew we didn't want to ask for more. I also knew we needed those washing machines and dryers. I spoke with the local dealer to get an idea of what the machines would cost as well as their service plans. It wouldn't do us any good if the machines broke down, and we couldn't get them serviced. I discovered we needed the heavy-duty, commercial coin-operated machines. We talked about financing, but the interest rates were high, and if I bought only four machines, I couldn't get as good a deal as a Laundromat that bought fifty to one hundred machines.

"We had a district meeting coming up, and I decided to see if any of the other managers had any ideas. They all agreed laundry facilities would be helpful, but no one knew where the money would come from. We all thought that surely once we had the machines, they would pay for themselves. If it was difficult to come up with the money for one Ronald McDonald House, it seemed impossible to raise enough for the twenty-five houses in the district. The district manager asked everyone to think about how we could raise money. She said that if anyone knew any bankers or finance types, we should tell them about our situation and see if they had any ideas.

"On the drive home, I thought of Coach. I wondered why he had talked about a dairy farm. Being a farm girl, I wanted to hear it. He might have some ideas on how to finance the washers and dryers, so I gave him a call.

"I said, 'Coach, I wondered why you were talking about a dairy farm. Also, we have permission to buy washers and dryers for the district as long as we pay for them and don't jeopardize our nonprofit status. I was wondering if you had any ideas on how to finance the machines.'

"Coach said, 'In regard to the dairy farm, I was talking about never-ending streams of income. For unending income, you need to think of a dairy farm instead of a milk cow...or a company that invests in bonds rather than an individual bond. In your case, it might help to think of a company that invests in washing machines like a Laundromat instead of an individual washing machine that wears out or depreciates until it needs to be replaced, just like a bond or a milk cow. Speaking of companies or funds that invest in bonds, the *Kiplinger* article may have been referring to them when it said that when interest rates go up, bonds go down. Of course, if the Federal Reserve announces an increase in interest rates, many companies will have a negative reaction including those that invest in bonds. However, an investor who uses a *bond co-op* or *bond laddering strategy* will see an increase in income during a rising-rate environment as bonds mature and funds are reinvested at higher interest rates. Bonds are fundamentally safer than common stocks.'

"I said, 'Coach, you just stated that bonds are fundamentally safer than stocks, and I've never heard that before. Why do you say that?'

"He said, 'There are a couple of reasons. First, *common stocks* are shares of ownership in a company, and *bonds* are debt obligations of a company. If a company goes bankrupt, and all the equipment and property are auctioned off, bondholders are paid first, and the common stock shareholders get anything that is left. Second, the dividends you receive from bond holdings are owed to you. Failure to pay your dividend in full and on time puts the company in default. A bond default is front-page news and negative for a company. If bondholders aren't paid, they will foreclose on a company and auction everything off if they have to.

"'Common stock dividends, on the other hand, are often much less reliable. The company can suspend or reduce dividends to shareholders without notice and for any reason. You'll be lucky if this gets any significant coverage or is even mentioned on television or the radio. If the company management wants to give themselves multimillion-dollar bonuses and jets for management training in the Caribbean instead of paying dividends, so sad, too bad for the common stock shareholder. Therefore, if you invest in bonds, your money is safer in case of bankruptcy. You are also more likely to receive your dividends in cases of poor stewardship or an economic downturn.'

"I said, 'That rings a bell. I remember my grandfather talking about a big, local employer that went bankrupt. The bondholders ended up getting their money back, but no one else got much of anything. I have heard of CD [*Certificate of Deposit*] laddering at the bank and credit union. For example, five-year CDs pay more than one-year CDs. You want the higher five-year yield but think that interest rates might be going up and do not want to tie up a large amount for five years. In a case like this, you could buy a $1,000, five-year CD every year for five years. You would have a five-year CD maturing every year after five years. If interest rates were going up, every year you could reinvest at a higher rate. Typically, someone would buy a one-, two-, three-, four-, and five-year CD at the same time. When the one-year CD comes due, you buy a five-year CD with it. When the two-year CD comes due, you buy a five-year CD with it. Every year when a CD comes due, you purchase another five-year CD until $5,000 is invested in five-year CDs. I was told if you do it this way, you can earn the five-year rate on all your CDs but still have access to some of the money every year without penalty. By using this laddering strategy, my income would be relatively stable even in unstable markets. It wouldn't matter whether interest rates were rising or falling, because I would be averaging in either way.'

"Coach said, 'That is correct. In fact, bonds are very much like CDs. CDs have traditionally been issued by banks and credit unions. Bonds are issued by both companies and governments. Bonds issued by companies are known as *corporate bonds* and generally are taxed. Bonds issued by states, cities, counties, and school, library, sewer, medical, and park districts are known as *municipal bonds.* Municipal bonds are usually free from federal income tax and sometimes state income tax.'

"I said, 'I did not know medical districts could issue tax-free bonds. Ronald McDonald House Charities is in a medical district. I don't recall hearing about companies that invest in bonds. Can you tell me about them and how they work?'

"He said, 'Think of them as a cooperative or a co-op for bonds. Are you familiar with co-ops?'

Marge put her hands on her hips, smiled big, and said, "Of course I am. I grew up on a farm!" Everyone laughed at that. She said, "FS is a farmer-owned cooperative that provides fuel, seeds, and grain bins to farmers. Coach said I was right once again. A *cooperative* is a group of people who voluntarily associate for their mutual benefit. A *mutual fund* is a type of co-op that pools money from many investors to purchase securities. Mutual funds are generally classified by the securities they own. The two main investment categories of mutual funds are bonds, also known as *fixed income funds,* and common stock, also known as *equity funds.* Funds that hold both stock and bond securities are called *hybrid funds.*

"Coach said, 'You could construct a longer-term bond ladder with individual bonds just like you do with CDs. It would be a little more complicated, because you would have to evaluate *credit risk*—that is, will they pay you back? CDs are considered risk-free, because banks and credit unions are insured. CDs are insured by the Federal Deposit Insurance Corporation (FDIC) for banks and by the National Credit Union Administration (NCUA) for credit unions.'

"I asked, 'Coach, why not just buy CDs if they are insured?'

"Coach said, 'You can, and many people keep some of their emergency money in CDs, but the return is so poor that it probably wouldn't keep up with inflation. *Inflation* is the rise in prices of things like rent, gas, food, and medical services over a period of time. I wouldn't consider it an investment. The interest rates on bonds, in general, are significantly higher than CDs.'

"I said, 'That's one of the main reasons I bought my bond instead of a CD. It pays more! Coach, how do you evaluate the credit risk on a bond?'

"Coach said, 'Bonds have credit ratings much like people have credit scores. You can go to the library and look up company and municipal bond ratings in Fitch, Moody's, or Standard & Poor's (S&P). The credit ratings are a lot like school grade cards—AAA, AA, A, BBB, BB, B, CCC, CC, C, and D for default! Triple-B ratings and up are generally considered to be investment grade, while double-B ratings and below are not. They are sometimes called high yield or junk bonds, but I think it is misleading to call them junk bonds. For example, the bond ratings for many companies making up the S&P 500 stock index are below investment grade, but are they called junk stocks? No, of course not, and people invest in the S&P 500 stock index without giving it a second thought. However, investing in S&P 500 bonds, which are safer and yield more, concerns them, and that is illogical. On top of that high-yield bonds tend to do well during a period of rising interest rates.'

"I asked, 'Why?'

"Coach said, 'Because, in general, rising rates imply an improving economy. If the economy is strengthening, some companies will have their bond ratings upgraded. When, for example, a BB bond is upgraded to a BBB, it becomes more valuable. This is one way bond co-ops make money in addition to simply collecting interest. They are often able to sell an upgraded bond for a profit, and this is known as a *capital gain*. This is why I value the bond co-op *distribution yield*, which is the money paid monthly to investors, over the *SEC [U.S. Securities and Exchange Commission] yield*, which is the hypothetical yield if all bonds are held to maturity.

'In fact, some bond co-ops even buy bonds in default. One example might be a fire that causes damage and shuts down production, resulting in a default and a drop in the bond price. The bond co-op could purchase the bond and, when the insurance check comes in, get all the back interest plus a capital gain when the bond is upgraded and sold.'

"Coach said he had some information from bond co-ops he had owned for years. I'm putting them up on the big screen so you can see them. These are from Vanguard and T. Rowe Price mutual fund companies. Coach said these big bond co-ops or bond mutual fund portfolios remind him of a CD ladder. As you can see, each fund has hundreds of bonds. At the time of these snapshots, interest rates were near all-time lows. These are both excellent funds and highly rated by Morningstar, an investment research firm."

T. Rowe Price Tax-Free High Yield Fund (PRFHX)

Percent of Total Net Assets by Credit Quality (523 Holdings)

AAA	2.1 percent
AA	5.9 percent
A	24.9 percent
BBB	35.4 percent
BB	7.1 percent
B	6.7 percent
CCC	0.5 percent
C	0.0 percent
D	1.7 percent
Not rated	15.8 percent

Vanguard High-Yield Tax-Exempt (VWAHX)

Distribution by Maturity (Percent of Fund) (1,018 Holdings)

Less than one year	10.7 percent
One to three years	9.2 percent
Three to five years	14.5 percent
Five to ten years	47.8 percent
Ten to twenty years	8.0 percent
Twenty to thirty years	7.2 percent
More than thirty years	2.6 percent
Total	100 percent

"If interest rates rise, the book value of a bond co-op could decline for a while, but as T. Rowe Price points out on their website, 'Although bond investors may incur some principal erosion as rates rise, the interest payments can be reinvested at the higher yields that become available. Over time, this can prove more rewarding than investing in short-term instruments that offer more principal protection but lower yields.'[2] In other words, as the bond co-ops' older, lower-interest rate bonds mature and are redeemed, new higher-interest rate bonds are purchased to replace them, and the bond co-ops' income increases. As the basket of bonds, also known as a *portfolio* of bonds, continues to provide increasing income, the bond co-ops' book value over time also increases. If the Federal Reserve raises interest rates and the price of a bond co-op drops, the price over time can be expected to recover and even exceed the price prior to the increase in interest rates.

"Here is a chart from the Yahoo Finance website comparing two municipal bond co-ops—T. Rowe Price Tax-Free High-Yield Fund (PRFHX) and Vanguard High-Yield Tax-Exempt Fund (VWAHX) to the S&P 500 stock index, which contains the largest five hundred companies in the country.

---

2 "Bond Strategies for Rising Interest Rates" T. Rowe Price Report Issue 120 Summer 2013, 7 http://individual.troweprice.com/staticFiles/Retail/Shared/PDFs/Summer2013PriceReport.pdf

AAAA[3]

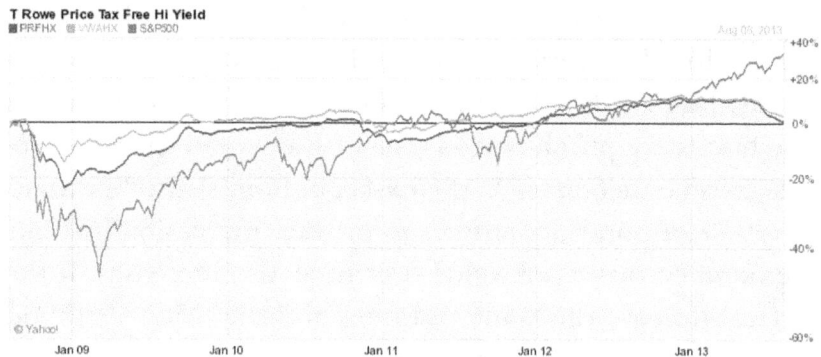

"As you can see, the bond co-op prices are much more stable than the common stock mutual fund. Note that these charts only show the stability of the price. They do not show the reinvested dividends. A ten-year chart including the re-invested dividends would show the value of the bond funds increasing significantly. The stability, safety, and tax-free nature of this type of bond mutual fund or bond co-op provides a good place to keep some emergency money. They are sleep-well-at-night funds. Another great thing about them is they pay monthly dividends that can be reinvested or directly deposited into a bank or credit union account.

"It's hard to beat a reliable, never-ending stream of tax-free, monthly income directly deposited into your account, wouldn't you agree?"

We all agree. I think Marge did a nice job of explaining tax-free municipal bonds.

---

3 "Five Year Interactive Chart T. Rowe Price Tax-Free High Yield (PRFHX)" Yahoo Finance accessed Aug 6, 2013 http://finance.yahoo.com/echarts?s=PRFHX+Interacti ve#symbol=PRFHX;range=5y

COOPERATIVES

Marge says, "I've learned that tax-free municipal bond mutual funds are hard to beat, but we plan to give them a run for the money with our widgets!"

Everyone applauds, and she says interested bidders should meet at the top of the hour in the Lincoln Room.

Chapter 14

THE HEAD

This is a good time to hit "the head" (a navy term for the restroom).

I've observed how important stability and monthly income is to the beginning investor who does "real work," regardless of age. Imagine a new investor, age twenty-five or fifty-five, who does real work for a living, and finally takes the plunge to invest three thousand hard-earned dollars in the S&P 500 stock index fund just before it takes a 40 percent drop.

What if it's worse than that? I need to tell my son about a friend at the gym, Kurt, whose company closed. It gave him his pension which was $75,000, and he took it, his lifetime savings, to a financial services firm. I remember him telling me he "couldn't lose," because he would own part of a large group of companies instead of just one that could go broke. I'm not sure he even received one dividend. His stock fund was down $30,000 within a matter of weeks. He said he had lost enough money and couldn't afford to lose any more.

He cashed out and put the money in CDs at the bank where he has earned next to nothing for over twenty years. I need to remind my kids to never invest in something they don't understand.

Imagine new investors seeing a stock fund dividend every three months instead of every month as with a bond fund. What if the money is tied up in some type of retirement savings program, or it declines in value by 40 percent, and the investors need the money? Do these negative factors help them sleep well at night? Are these factors going to help them reach their tipping point? My experience in helping beginning investors suggests that the answer is no.

I have read and agree with the advice to not invest in common stocks if the money might be needed in the next five years. I believe if you are within five years of retirement, and you have the opportunity to sell the stock funds in your retirement plan at an attractive price, you should do it. You don't want to mess up and delay your retirement! I recall hearing people say they were in the stock market for the long haul. However, the market had been up several years in a row and was expensive by historical standards. They were planning to retire in two years! How does the old saying go? "Bulls win, bears win, hogs get slaughtered."

I felt bad for them, because they couldn't afford to retire, and their dreams were put on hold. The stock market can go down and stay down for years. Do you want to delay your retirement until the stock market recovers? Does the beginning investor want to sell at a loss because the cash is needed? Let us consider the following from the Fidelity Family of Mutual Funds:

As the bear market of 2008 to 2009 showed, a market downturn may deliver a nasty blow to your savings when you are just beginning retirement—a blow that might have lifestyle-changing implications. In fact, because of financial concerns, 60% of workers over 60 plan to seek another job after retiring from their present company. In addition, 11% of workers in this age bracket don't think they will ever be able to retire.[4]

One advantage mutual funds have is their dividends can be reinvested without any brokerage fees. Additional contributions of one hundred dollars or more can also be made without any brokerage fees. Many investors use a system called *dollar cost averaging*. With this system you contribute an identical amount of money every month (for example, one hundred dollars). By purchasing one hundred dollars each month when the price is high, you will be getting fewer shares for your money, and when prices are low, you will be getting more shares for your money. Over time, you will end up with a lower average price per share and a higher average return. This is an especially helpful strategy for stock mutual funds, because they are more unstable. They bob up and down in price, which is called *volatility*.

This reminds me of an interview with Jack Bogle, the founder of Vanguard Funds:

---

4 "Safeguard your retirement income" *Fidelity Viewpoints* June 26, 2013 www.fidelity. com/viewpoints/retirement/safeguard-retirement-savings

This gives me an opportunity to make my other idea about retirement clear. That is, we're all transfixed with the movements of the stock market; up and down, up and down, up and down, when that has nothing to do with your retirement, zero. What you should be looking at is the stream of income…And as long as you get those checks, your retirement plan is unaffected. You don't care whether it's worth a lot or a little as long as the checks come in…in the long run focus on the dividend stream…think about your retirement in terms of when you go out to that little old mailbox and pull out…envelopes, your fund envelope and your government envelope and maybe another pension plan or something, whatever there is, and that's what should matter to you in retirement…corporate America needs a lot of cleanup, a sweeping out. Executive compensation is a disgrace.[5]

I agree, it is a disgrace, especially when they haven't been paying dividends! In fact, in my opinion, stocks that do not pay a dividend are no better than collectables. They do not provide any income or reduce your expenses. The only way you can get any money out of them is to sell them.

Besides the stability of bond mutual fund prices and dividends, new investors can enjoy additional monthly income almost immediately. They can see their account balance and income rise just about every month, especially if they are making additional monthly contributions. Stock mutual

5   David Van Knapp, "Bogle's Views on Retirement Income" *Seeking Alpha* July 18, 2013 http://seekingalpha.com/article/1556142-bogles-views-on-retirement-income

funds and bond mutual funds remind me of Aesop's fable of the hare and the tortoise. Stock mutual funds can race ahead only to change direction and race to the rear. Bond funds are more like the tortoise, making stable and steady progress. Perhaps it might help to think of bond funds as the football team that keeps the ball on the ground, makes first downs, and maintains possession of the ball. Stock funds are more like the teams that pass all the time and have interceptions and turnovers. Bond funds are like a baseball player who is happy to get on base with a single or a double and almost always does. Stock funds are like the players who swing for the fence, don't get on base that much, but occasionally hit a home run.

Of course, personal finances are not a game. When I think of financial storms, I think of job loss, hospitalizations, hurricanes, tornadoes, fires, or floods that have the potential to destroy everything you have. If you are on a ship at sea in a hurricane, would you rather be on the USS *John F. Kennedy* (CV-67), an aircraft carrier, or on a fast little destroyer escort? Don't forget the flight deck of the USS *John F. Kennedy* is about six stories high off the water.

At the Navy Club, I recall hearing stories that in September of 1999, during Hurricane Floyd, the USS *John F. Kennedy* had waves breaking over the flight deck. It and several other ships had been ordered out to sea to avoid the storm. Satellite images showed the carrier safely out of harm's way but heroically turning back into the storm to rescue the eight-man crew from the sinking 150-foot *Gulf Majesty*. Captain Mike Miller had two choices: keep his boat and thousands of crew safely out of harm's way and let the *Gulf Majesty* crew die or sail directly into the hurricane. The ship and crew of the USS *John F. Kennedy* bravely sailed through three hundred miles of high seas to the most dangerous part of the storm near the center.[6] Note I said bravely—I didn't say they weren't scared. The crew described how the deck heaved so violently they feared the keel would break. I'm proud to have served on the USS *John F. Kennedy*, and this reminds me of a quote.

My work in financial policy research and analysis took me to Washington, DC, on a couple of occasions. It is one of the most special, beautiful, and pedestrian-friendly places I've ever been. After long days of sitting in meetings, I enjoyed taking walks. I happened upon what felt like a sacred place: the Navy Memorial. On it was a quote from our thirty-fifth president and a World War II Patrol Torpedo (PT) boat commander, John F. Kennedy: "And any man who may be asked, what he did to make his life worthwhile, I think can respond with a good deal of pride and satisfaction: 'I served in the United States Navy.'"

Municipal bond funds have increased stability much like an 80,000-ton aircraft carrier that is over one-thousand-feet long. A stock fund is less stable—more like a destroyer escort weighing two thousand tons and three-hundred-feet long, bobbing up and down on the waves. Not only are municipal bonds one of the safest and most stable investments, but I

---

6 Joseph A Gambardello, "In Harrowing High-seas Rescue, Tugboat Crew Pulled To Safety An Aircraft Carrier Found The Eight, Who Had Abandoned Ship. Three Of Them Floated In Lifejackets For 5½ Hours" *The Inquirer* September 16, 1999 http://articles.philly. com/1999-09-16/news/25488832_1_aircraft-carrier-high-seas-rescue-flight-deck.

feel good about what my municipal bond investments are supporting: libraries, schools, hospitals, clean water, roads, and bridges here in the good old United States of America. Municipal bond funds tend to have lower volatility than even other types of bond funds because of their tax-free status for US citizens. Corporate and treasury bonds are purchased by everyone, including foreign governments and companies. No discussion of bond stability or lack thereof would be complete without the mention of emerging market bonds and another old saying I've heard for years. Why do they call them "emerging markets?" Because, of course, that's where emergencies happen! This includes things like military coups and financial collapse.

When you are investing in bonds, remember you are lending money. There are plenty of companies, states, cities, villages, and counties here in the United States with bond ratings that need your investment and will pay you back with interest. As an investor, I sleep better knowing that if any problems were to arise, I have the best legal system in the world on my side. In Dixon, Illinois, a government employee stole millions of dollars over a period of years. She got caught, and it took years to locate all her ill-gotten gain and auction off her race horses, jewelry, stables, boats, and airplanes. If I recall correctly, the legal system recovered over fifty million dollars! This is why bonds here in the United States are fundamentally safer: you are owed the money, and our legal system is excellent when it comes to protecting investors. What happens if you loan your hard-earned money overseas, and a foreign government has a crisis? Take a guess. I can imagine a gentle shrug of the shoulders and a sheepish grin saying, "No understand English. So sad, too bad, go home Yankee!"

If a personal financial storm hits, a mutual fund investor can take one of several steps, depending on the severity of the situation. First, you could stop contributions at any time but continue to reinvest the dividends. Second, you could cancel the reinvestment of dividends and have the dividends deposited into a bank or credit union account. Third, if these actions are not sufficient to weather the storm, and there is a need to sell, you can have the cash within a few days. The municipal bond fund's tax-free status, credit quality, stability, safety, yield, and *liquidity* (the ability to turn an asset into cash quickly) make them a good place to keep some of your emergency funds.

One suggestion is to keep three months of income (or half of your emergency money) in different insured accounts: one at your bank and one at your credit union. The other half of your emergency money could be in two different bond co-ops, each having low expenses and initial investment requirements. Two good examples are the funds previously shown. The T. Rowe Price Tax-Free High Yield Fund (PRFHX) and the Vanguard High-Yield Tax-Exempt Fund (VWAHX) both have excellent track records over a quarter of a century long.

A common rule of thumb is to have at least six months of expenses in an emergency fund, but I also think in terms of income. If your annual income or expenses are $20,000, you want to have at least $10,000 in an emergency fund before investing in common stocks.

It wouldn't hurt to keep reinvesting the dividends in your municipal bond mutual fund accounts or bond co-ops until you have two years of income in an emergency fund. Imagine having two years of income in your municipal bonds. You would not only have a great sleep well at night emergency fund but a tax-free income stream for life. My goal was to have at least enough tax-free municipal bond income to pay my property taxes and enough regulated utility income to cover my utility bills. Two of the most reliable and safest streams of unearned income you can find are regulated utilities and municipal bonds. Life starts to look considerably better to working people once they have a well-insulated home that is paid off and some extra money coming in to help with the property taxes and utility bills. They are well on their way to hitting their tipping point!

I had better get to the Lincoln Room. I don't want to miss out on the presentation and the chance to bid on the widgets!

Chapter 15

THE LINCOLN ROOM

I see that a few of us are early, and there is my American Legion buddy and former coworker, Scott, talking to Jim, Linda, and Bob. Scott and I did the same job for years before we received promotions and retired as program planners. He was a marine who received his master's in business administration after he was discharged. He is also a certified financial planner. The best thing about certified financial planners is they are paid by the hour or the job, like an attorney, rather than by commission like an insurance or stock seller. The advice they give you is less likely to pose a conflict of interest. In other words, you are not being "pitched" the product that gives the salesperson the highest commission. You have hired a professional who will look out for your best interest and explain the advantages and disadvantages of various options.

If you win the lotto or a big race, have a hit album, play in the World Series, inherit money, or receive a large amount of overtime, seriously consider talking to a certified financial planner. You would be lucky to find someone like Scott. I've learned a lot from him through the years, and when I told him I owned rental properties but wasn't sure if I wanted any more, he understood. It was probably twenty-five years ago when he told me about *real estate investment trusts* (REITs).

Linda and I taught a class together. I knew I liked her the first time I saw her office. She had worked at the nonprofit credit counseling agency for five years and had on her wall the following scripture from Psalm 37:21: "The wicked borrows and does not repay, but the righteous shows mercy and gives." It was appropriate for her work at the nonprofit credit counseling agency, and I learned about it from my first tenants, newlyweds almost thirty years ago. Everything was great until the husband was laid off from the local heavy equipment manufacturer. They did not want to leave their first home and held off as long as possible before moving in with Mom. The rent wasn't the only bill they owed, and their credit was down the tubes.

I received a phone call from the nonprofit credit counseling agency. The credit counselor told me she had reviewed my former tenant's financial information, and it was her understanding that they owed me two month's rent. I said yes. She asked me if I would be interested in being paid for those two months of rent. She asked me, a landlord, if I was interested in being paid back rent. Of course I wanted to be paid the money owed to me. She said they had enrolled in their program, and all their income would go directly to the agency, and the agency would pay all their bills for them. She was authorized to issue me a check *today* for seventy-five dollars and every month for eleven more months until the debt of $900 was paid off. Was this acceptable?

I said I preferred to have the entire amount. They had owed me the money for some time, and I asked if there were any other options.

She said that, unfortunately, there were none. She said they felt terrible they hadn't been able to pay what they owed. Their situation was improving in that they had both been able to find part-time jobs, and their goal was to pay off their bills. She understood that "all of the creditors" wanted their money now, but it simply wasn't possible. This is why they had enrolled in the program.

She said, "I can have your check in the mail today, and you should have it in a couple of days. Do you want me to make out a check to you, or do you wish to engage the services of an attorney? I believe that would be a waste of everyone's time, because the judge is going to see their limited income and that they are making a good faith effort to pay off all their creditors." I chose the check.

"Do you understand that by endorsing and cashing the check, you have agreed to the plan as I have proposed?"

"Yes," I said, and we were off the phone. I had questioned the nonprofit credit counselor, and she passed with flying colors. I felt my former tenants were in good hands, and I was impressed with her performance. If I ran into anyone else in their situation, I knew where to refer them.

I've also referred people to Scott. I refer to him people I meet who have a combination investment/life insurance policy, often known as *whole life insurance.* Sometimes people have been paying whole life insurance premiums for decades, and even though they are poor investments, because they have been paying on them so long, it is better to keep them than cancel.

When Scott told me that sometimes the only real option with some investment/life insurance policies is to borrow your own money back from them, I said, "What?"

I remember him saying with a grin, "Of course, it's at a very reasonable interest rate."

I told him, "I would hope so, borrowing your own money and paying interest on it. What will the insurance companies think of next?"

I knew early on that term insurance was the least expensive type of life insurance and the best option for my family. Every parent with young children should have at least enough life insurance to pay off their debts and help their kids with school. The odds are that it will never be needed, but if something should happen, your family won't be left destitute. This reminds me of the old saying: "Buy term and invest the difference." For example, if an investment/life insurance policy or whole life policy costs $115 per month, and a term life insurance policy costs fifteen dollars per month, you are better off purchasing the fifteen-dollar policy and putting one hundred dollars toward your mortgage or in a *no-load* (no sales commission), low-expense mutual fund such as those you find with Vanguard, T. Rowe Price, and Fidelity mutual fund families.

As I approach, I hear Linda say, "What!" and I say hello to everyone.

Scott just said, "A dollar saved is *not* a dollar earned."

Linda turns to Scott and says, "Tell us how a dollar saved is *not* a dollar earned."

I can see Scott is treading on thin ice with her. Linda works with a lot of "spend-a-holics," and the only way they "save" is what they "save" at a sale when they buy something. One of Linda's daily struggles is trying to convey the importance of saving for a rainy day. With many of her clients, it is like trying to lead a mule to water. It is clear she isn't buying what Scott is saying.

Scott says, "Because a dollar saved is worth *more* than a dollar earned!"

Linda says, "How can that be?"

"It's because of taxes. If you consider taxes, a dollar saved is worth at least one dollar and twenty cents. For example, in order to purchase a one-dollar tomato, I have to earn at least one dollar and twenty cents. The federal government will take at least fifteen cents, and the state government will take five cents off the top in taxes, before I get my dollar to purchase a tomato. If I grow a tomato, although it would cost me one dollar at the grocery store, it would really be worth one dollar and twenty cents to me."

"That is an interesting way to look at it."

Jim says, "Hey, Coach, I remember that. That's what you said when I was thinking about replacing my single-pane windows with energy-efficient ones. If the windows save me one hundred dollars per year in heating and cooling bills, it is like saving $120 per year when you consider it like tax-free income."

Bob says, "I never thought of reduced recurring expenses as tax-free income, but I see your point. That's an excellent way to look at it. Energy-efficient windows are like tax-free, money-making machines."

We all agree. You can think of double-pane, energy-efficient windows as unearned, tax-free, money-making machines like solar panels on your roof. You can think of energy-efficient appliances and air conditioning and heating the same way. Fuel-efficient vehicles and insulating your house fall into the same category.

As we stand there talking, I realize that between Linda, Scott and I, we could advise the complete economic spectrum. Linda helps people who are behind on their bills and have credit problems. My focus is helping working people hit their tipping point and early retirement. Scott is there for those more fortunate who had received a large amount of money and those unfortunate enough to have become entangled in an investment/life insurance policy. It is not inexpensive to hire a certified financial planner, but if you've lost a spouse or a surviving parent, and your inheritance is significantly more than your debts, you should consider talking to someone like Scott. A certified financial planner will put your entire estate and recommendations in a binder for you. When I last checked, the cost was between $500 and $1,500 and under one hundred dollars for an investment/life insurance policy analysis.

"Hey, Coach," says Scott, "I saw this article and thought of you. I know you like to describe the bond co-ops as aircraft carriers, and in this Brad Thomas article on *Seeking Alpha*, he describes real estate investment trusts as battleships." He hands me a copy. Brad wrote,

"Ralph Block, in his book *Investing in REITs*, explains 'blue chip' REIT shares:"

The blue chip REITs take you safely through the ups and downs…and deliver consistent, rising, long-term growth in…dividends…They are financially strong and widely respected…They will not always provide the highest dividend yields or even, in many years, the best total returns, nor can you buy them at bargain prices—but they should provide years of double-digit returns with a high degree of safety…and will provide very satisfying returns.

"I often describe blue chip REITs as battleships since they are better prepared for the future risks and they are perhaps even stronger after experiencing the effects of difficult times."[7]

I say, "This is interesting, great minds think alike" as I hand the article to Bob.

Scott says, "I thought you would like it."

"What do you have there, Bob?" Marge says as she joins us.

"It's an article about blue chip real estate investment trusts being like battleships. I've heard of trusts, but I haven't heard about real estate investment trusts."

---

7 Brad Thomas, "Is Now The Time To Double Down In REIT Town?" *Seeking Alpha* August 19, 2013 http://seekingalpha.com/article/1643042-is-now-the-time-to-double-down-in-reit-town

"I haven't either. What are they?"

Scott says, "Real estate investment trusts [REITs] were approved by Congress in the 1960s to provide a new way for people to invest in real estate. People have always been able to invest in real estate through direct ownership of houses, buildings, or land, but with this legislation, they can form "real estate co-ops," to borrow a term from Coach, to purchase buildings or land. It provides a tax-efficient way for average working people to own, for example, part of an apartment complex, office building, shopping mall, warehouse, or forest. In order to qualify as an REIT, the co-op must invest a majority of assets in real estate, derive a majority of income from real estate, and most importantly, according to Coach, *must distribute at least 90 percent of the taxable income to shareholders in the form of dividends.*"

Bob says, "What, did I hear you correctly? A real estate co-op or REIT will do all the property and tenant selection, rent collection, maintenance, evictions, plumbing, carpentry, and heating and cooling repairs, but I still get 90 percent of the taxable income?"

"That's correct, and if you hold your REIT in a Roth IRA [Individual Retirement Account], the income is tax-free." says Scott.

I see the wheels turning in Bob's head as he considers the potential. He is probably wondering if this is his ticket to freedom from taxes, backed up toilets, and deadbeat tenants.

Marge says, "My tax accountant told me the smartest thing I could do for myself is open a Roth account. She said the money would grow in the account tax-free for the rest of my life."

Scott says, "I agree with your accountant! Opening a Roth IRA is one of the wisest financial moves you can make."

Bob asks, "I've wondered about that. Can't you deduct your contribution from your taxable income and lower your tax bill?"

Scott says," I think you are referring to a traditional IRA. With a traditional IRA, for example, if you earn $50,000 per year and make a contribution of $5,000, you can subtract the $5,000 from your taxable income and pay taxes on $45,000. In a traditional IRA, your money grows over time, and any taxes due on interest or dividends are *tax-deferred*. Tax-deferred means you pay taxes on the money when you withdraw it from the account. One of the key differences with the Roth IRA is you have already paid the taxes on your contributions, and any future interest or dividends are *tax-free*." Bob says, "I didn't realize that. There is a huge difference between tax-deferred and tax-free."

I say, "You can say that again. In my opinion, the only time a traditional IRA makes sense is when you are near the end of your career in a high tax bracket, and you're expecting to be in a lower tax bracket once you retire. For younger people, the Roth IRA is superior to a traditional IRA. It's much better to pay 15 percent on a $5,000 contribution rather than pay, for example, 25 percent on hundreds of thousands of dollars later in life when taking your mandatory distributions."

Scott says, "I agree. Coach brings up another important advantage of the Roth IRA: mandatory distributions. With a traditional IRA, you must start taking mandatory distributions at age seventy and a half. With a Roth IRA, you are never forced to withdraw your money. Your money is there if you need it in your twilight years, or you can even leave it as part of your estate."

Marge says, "It sure seems like the Roth IRA is a better option for me. Coach, did you say hundreds of thousands of dollars, how would you do that?"

I say, "What did Albert Einstein say? 'Compound interest is the eighth wonder of the world. He who understands it, earns it ... he who doesn't ... pays it.'"

Marge says, "I want to learn about that, but it looks like my boss is ready for me to make some announcements. I'll be back!"

I say, "Marge, I have a spreadsheet that I think will help explain compound interest and how people are able to accumulate hundreds of thousands of dollars. It's out in my Jeep. I'll go get it."

"We'd like to see it too," the others say.

Chapter 16

THE ANNOUNCEMENT

Marge says, "I know everyone is anxious to find out the details on the widgets. We are going to have a silent auction in order to set the price. This program is being organized as a 'tax-free mini municipal bond nonprofit cooperative,' and the official name for the mystery widgets is McBonds. They are for the exclusive benefit of Ronald McDonald House Charities guests and volunteers. Bids will be accepted for a minimum of ten McBonds. This means every successful bidder will receive at least five dollars or twenty quarters per month in tax-free income."

"You've probably been wondering how you are going to receive your money. You will receive a card, much like this McDonalds gift card, that will automatically be credited with your monthly tax-free income based on the number of McBonds you purchased. You may redeem your money in three different ways. First, you can go into your local Ronald McDonalds House Charities, swipe your card in the laundry room, and receive your money in quarters."

The crowd went *hmmm* as people absorbed the concept.

"Secondly, the card can be used at any one of the thousands of McDonalds to purchase their delicious products. On top of that, McDonalds Corporation has agreed to contribute one cent for every dollar in card purchases to Ronald McDonald House Charities."

This draws applause from everyone, including me!

"Last, especially for those who are considering bidding on larger quantities of McBonds or have kids at home or in college, you can redeem your monthly income by purchasing McDonalds gift cards. Isn't that great?"

Everyone nods in agreement and applauds.

Now that Marge has the crowd worked up, she says, "The bid forms are over there. Please enter your bid on ten or more McBonds, and remember that it's for a good cause. The executive staff will review the bids and make an announcement as to the prices and the winning bids. Good luck everyone!"

Chapter 17

THE BID

Now is a good time to go outside and get the spreadsheet I've been working on as well as some other helpful articles. The spreadsheet took some time to do, and I think it will help people to understand the concept of compound interest.

I also want to think about my bid. I know if I bid $1,000 for ten McBonds, it would be five dollars monthly [10 x .50 = $5]. This would work out to 6 percent [.06 x $1,000 = $60 per year, and $60 / 12 months = $5 per month]. Because I've been earning 6 percent tax-free on average from my bond funds and over 7 percent tax-free on the REITs in my Roth, I don't want to receive less than 6 percent. Because interest rates and inflation have been trending up, I should be receiving payment increases over time with my bond funds and REITs. I also have the advantage of automatically reinvesting my dividends each month, so my money is compounding that much faster.

However, this is for a good cause, and I do go to McDonalds regularly. If there is any leftover money, I can cash it out when I volunteer at Ronald McDonald House Charities. It would help cover the cost for the food I contribute. If I can get forty McBonds for $4,000, that will be twenty dollars per month tax-free. All things considered, it would work for me. I will bid $4,000 for forty McBonds—$4,000 will help buy some washers and dryers!

It looks like everyone in our group has put in their bid, and they are standing there waiting for me. I'll give them the information sheet and place my bid.

"This is the spreadsheet showing how compound interest works and some other articles I thought you might find interesting too. Why don't you look them over while I place my bid?"

"Sounds good," they say.

"One quick note, this spreadsheet shows what will happen if you start a bond fund account with an opening balance of $3,000, contribute one hundred per month, and reinvest your dividends. It shows how your money will grow. It's pretty amazing. In less than five years, you have over $10,000 and are earning over fifty dollars per month. Just think what it would be if you put in $458 per month! It is at a 6 percent interest rate, which means that you are earning a half a percent per month [.06 / 12=.005]. I also replicated the spreadsheet in a chart format."

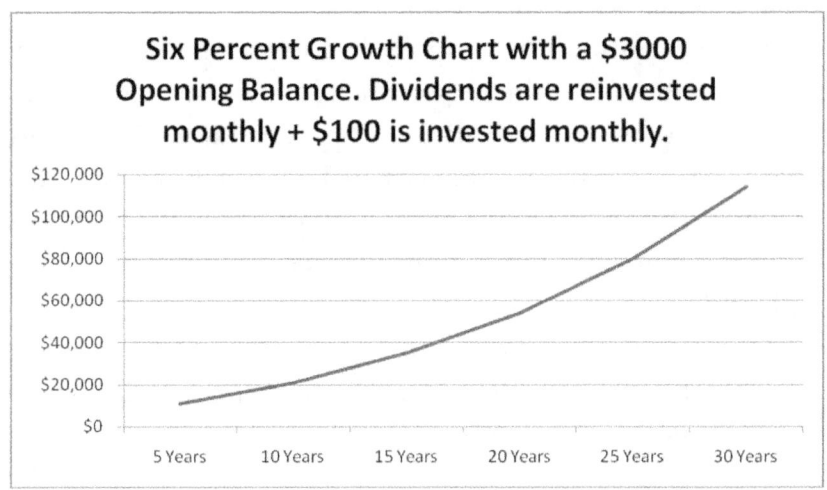

Six Percent Growth Chart with a $3000 Opening Balance. Dividends are reinvested monthly + $100 is invested monthly.

[Note: The source spreadsheet is located in the Appendix]

"This is amazing," says Linda. She hands the spreadsheet to Marge as I rejoin the group.

"You can say that again," says Jim.

"I haven't shown this to my son or daughter yet," I say, "but I'm hoping it will help them understand the power of compound interest and the importance of funding a Roth account, the sooner the better. I heard Mark Cortazzo, in an interview on the Consuelo Mack WEALTHRACK public television program, state that if a young person contributes $5,500 per year [$5,500 / 12 = $458.33 per month, currently the legal maximum for someone under the age of fifty] for ten years and then stops, the money grows to over 1.5 million dollars by the time the person is sixty-five. He described compounding money inside a Roth IRA as very powerful and the ultimate tax shelter![8] I agree with Mark. In my opinion, monthly dividend-paying, high-yield bond funds [co-ops] and REITs parked inside a Roth IRA are probably the most stable, reliable, and powerful method the average working person has to accumulate and create real wealth."

Marge says, "Coach, I think you've answered my question. It is possible for someone like me to accumulate hundreds of thousands of dollars. Wow!"

---

8 Consuelo Mack, "Cortazzo & Lebenthal Minimizing Tax Pain" *WEALTHTRACK* December 13, 2013 http://wealthtrack.com/recent-programs/premium-mark-cortazzo-alexandra-lebenthal-2/

Chapter 18

Q AND A

Bob says, "I always heard that putting stock mutual funds in an IRA was the way to go and that over the long haul, stocks do better."

"Better watch out, Bob," Scott says with a smile, "you're treading on thin ice with Coach."

"Scott's right," I say. "This is one of my hot buttons for a few reasons. Nothing irritates me more than senior management giving themselves multimillion-dollar pay packages and benefit increases, while at the same time telling employees that they must cut their salaries, pension, dental, and health benefits. On top of that, they want to pay the common stock shareholders peanuts in the form of dividends. So, in general, I prefer income-producing assets such as bonds, regulated utility stocks, and REITs. This is my opinion based on experience. However, I did bring an excerpt from an article Dr. Donald van Deventer wrote. It was published on *Seeking Alpha*. Does anyone have that?"

"I was just looking at it," Linda says as she hands it to Bob. "It's excellent."

"I agree. He has a PhD in business economics from Harvard and coauthored some books on financial risk analysis."

Don't believe the assertion that "In the long run stocks outperform fixed income securities"

This is a common mantra of people who get paid a commission selling common stock. At a convention in Geneva in December 2004, Nobel Laureate Robert C. Merton told a joke that goes something like this: "An equity salesman for a major Wall Street firm called on a very conservative pension fund manager, who had invested 100% of the pension fund's assets in fixed income securities. The equity salesman told him, 'Why don't you shift your portfolio into common stock? In the long run, you'll have a 99% probability of having more money because your time horizon is so long.' The pension fund manager replied, 'Well, if you are right, your firm would find it very inexpensive to provide me with a portfolio insurance policy that will pay me the difference if ever an all equity portfolio was worth less than my fixed income portfolio is worth today. Why don't you price that insurance policy with your colleagues and call me back? If it's as cheap as your argument indicates it should be, I am sure your firm will offer me that insurance policy very cheaply.'" As Merton's audience laughed, he added (of course) that the salesman never called back, because the risk of equity portfolio price declines is huge and such an insurance policy would also be very expensive. Some people just don't believe this, so here's just one example of how big the risk is. The Nikkei 225 stock index traded at almost 39,000 at the end of 1989. Today, 24 years later, the index is at 13,460. One should remember that as recently as 2005, commentators were arguing that home prices in the U.S. could never fall like they did in the collapse of the Japanese bubble.[9]

Bob says, "This is an interesting read."

"I thought you would think so," I say. "With regard to placing common stocks inside your Roth, I have a piece from Fidelity Investments that discusses this topic, and I think it is well written. Who has that?"

"I do," says Jim as he finishes reading and hands the article to Bob.

There's another companion strategy that many investors often overlook. Known as "asset location," it involves strategically positioning investments in taxable, tax-deferred, or tax-free accounts to potentially help minimize the overall tax hit to your portfolio. For example, most taxable bonds generate interest, which is taxed at ordinary income rates. So, you may want to consider holding such bonds in traditional IRAs or 401(k)s, where interest income is tax deferred, or in Roth-type accounts, where interest is

---

9   Donald Van Deventer, "Straight Talk: 6 Candid Rules For Individual Investors" *Seeking Alpha* August 29, 2013 http://seekingalpha.com/article/1665572-straight-talk-6-candid-rules-for-individual-investors

federally tax-free, if certain conditions are met. By contrast, stocks that you plan to own long term are often better held in taxable accounts, because gains are taxed at long-term capital gains rates, which are generally lower than ordinary income tax rates.[10]

Bob says, "This is thought provoking and puzzling."

Jim says, "Hey, Coach, tell him about the storage sheds. That's how I learned it."

"Okay. I like to explain it in terms of storage space. Say that you have a closet in your home that you use for storage. You also have a shed that you use for storage. The shed is much larger and can hold a lot, but it's not climate controlled. Your closet is, so you put in it items, such as pictures that cannot tolerate temperature extremes.

"Think of your Roth IRA as your climate-controlled closet. Because a Roth IRA has such special features, the government limits the amount of money you can put in it every year. Currently, for a young single person, the limit is $5,500 per year. Because space is limited in the Roth IRA, I believe the assets that should be put in there should only be high-dividend or income assets that do not receive favored tax treatment by the government. The only assets I keep in my Roth IRA are taxable corporate bond co-ops and REITs.

"In my taxable accounts, the shed, I hold assets that are tax advantaged and have lower yields such as tax-free municipal bonds and common stocks. Why would you hold tax-free municipal bonds in a Roth? It would be illogical.

---

10 "How to efficiently turn savings into income" *Fidelity Viewpoints* July 24, 2013 https://www.fidelity.com/viewpoints/retirement/savings-to-income

They are already earning dividends and compounding on a monthly, tax-free basis. Keeping a tax-free municipal bond fund in your Roth would make about as much sense as keeping a garden hoe in the house and your broom out in the shed."

"That's a good one," says Marge, laughing.

Jim says, "Yes, Coach has a way of explaining things so you can understand them."

Linda asks, "Coach, what funds or REITs do you like?"

"There are several REITs that pay monthly dividends, but one of the oldest, largest, and most reliable dividend payers is the Realty Income Company known as The Monthly Dividend Company (O). It has been paying monthly dividends for over forty years and has had over seventy dividend increases in the last twenty years. Unfortunately, it does not allow for a Roth in its dividend reinvestment program (DRIP), but you can accomplish the same thing through programs like Scott Trade's Flexible Reinvestment program. I've held a couple of high-yield bond co-ops in my Roth account since before the financial markets crashed in 2008, and I've been happy with their performance. The two funds are T. Rowe Price's Corporate High Yield Fund (PRHYX) and Vanguard's Corporate High Yield Fund (VWEHX). In my taxable account, I've held the T. Rowe Price Tax-Free High Yield Fund (PRFHX) and the Vanguard High-Yield Tax-Exempt Fund (VWAHX), also since before the crash. Whether the financial seas are calm or raging, these four aircraft carriers and battleship have sailed admirably.

They have paid monthly dividends every month, and the dividends just keep growing, as you see on the spreadsheet."

Bob says, "If I understand you and these articles correctly, you are not a big fan of purchasing common stocks and putting them in your Roth. Is that correct?"

"That is correct. Common stocks are taxed at the qualified dividend tax rate (QDTR), so for people in the 10–15 percent income tax bracket, their QDTR is zero! Even for those in the 25–35 percent income tax bracket, their QDTR is currently only 15 percent. Because we have to pay regular taxes on corporate bonds and REITs, I believe they should be your first choice for your Roth account."

"Haven't some people made fortunes trading in common stocks?" asks Bob. "What do you recommend?"

"Some people have made fortunes timing the market and trading common stocks, but don't forget that people have also lost fortunes. However, for the average small investor, I prefer purchasing common stocks, such as utility stocks directly from a company, and participating in its DRIP program. Over the long haul, it's hard to beat dollar-cost averaging through the systematic reinvestment of dividends, coupled with the ability to make commission-free additional investments.

I suppose you could also consider holding a basket of high-dividend stocks or dividend-growth stocks in a taxable account through an exchange traded fund (EFT) instead of a mutual fund, especially if you are with a broker that has a no-commission reinvestment program for the quarterly dividends. I believe ETFs have some advantages over equity mutual funds in a taxable account. Fidelity has a special relationship with iShares, and there are a number of ETFs you can buy or sell without paying a commission. That being said, I think beginning investors who haven't hit their tipping point yet are going to be happier and more successful with the steadily growing monthly dividends they can receive from bond mutual funds."

Scott says, "That reminds me of an interview I watched on Consuelo Mac's Wealth Track with Christine Benz and Russel Kinnel of Morningstar. Morningstar did a study, and it showed that individual, small investors tend to buy and sell at the exact wrong times, and thus they tend to underperform the mutual funds or ETFs they invest in. For example, they tend to buy when the market has been rising, wanting to get in on a good thing, and sell when the market is down, not wanting to lose any more money.

"Evidently, target-date retirement funds work well for many average and inexperienced investors. They can go to their favorite mutual fund family such as T. Rowe Price, Fidelity, or Vanguard and pick out the date they plan to retire. All they have to do is make their monthly contributions, which are automatically invested in a well-diversified portfolio of domestic stocks, foreign stocks, foreign bonds, and domestic bonds that rebalance over time. From a psychological standpoint, this works for many people, and they are able to avoid making emotional mistakes.[11] What do you think, Coach?"

---

11 Consuelo Mack, "Benz & Kinnel" *WEALTHTRACK* November 15, 2013 http://wealthtrack.com/recent-programs/benz-kinnel-mutual-fund-shakeups/

I say, "I didn't see the interview, but I've read that these types of hybrid funds are gaining in popularity. I like the fact that they are well diversified and automatically rebalance themselves. I can see for many people this could be a good way to go, especially if it's in a program offered at work and if the company matches part of the contribution. It's working for some people when other strategies don't seem to click for them. However, I like keeping all my money safe and sound in the good old United States of America!"

Scott says, "I understand your feelings on that, Coach, but let's not forget about some great foreign companies such as Nestle, Bayer, Royal Dutch Shell, Sony, BMW, Mercedes, Honda, Electrolux, Fiat, and Toyota."

"Point well taken," I say.

Marge says, "Hanging around you guys is a real education. Looks like they want me back on the stage. Good luck on your McBond bids!"

Chapter 19

THE RESULTS

Marge has been in the office with the top management for some time, and we are wondering what the delay is. I've been wondering if my $4,000 bid for forty McBonds will be accepted.

Here comes Marge, and she looks concerned. I hope she's not disappointed with the bids. Surely, with this group of people, we were able to raise enough money to buy a few washers and dryers for one of the most worthy causes I know, Ronald McDonald House Charities!

"Hi again, everyone," she says. "You've probably been wondering what we've been doing, and you're never going to believe it. I'm still in shock. We've been doing arithmetic and been on the phone to HQ. We have encountered a problem that never occurred to us. We have been banging our heads together, trying to figure out how to solve it. We've come to a decision we hope will not offend anyone and will be the best decision for the highest number of volunteers. Let me emphasize that we treasure and value every one of you. I wish to remind everyone we are a nonprofit organization doing noble work, and we request your understanding in this matter."

I'm beginning to think something is seriously wrong, and the whole thing is going up in smoke.

"First, the good news," she says. "We hit our goal! We will be able to purchase all the washing machines and dryers needed for our district!"

Everyone applauds, and I'm glad. That's the most important thing. I can live without the McBonds.

"The bad news is that, to my amazement, we have bids for more McBonds than we can sell tonight. In fact, a few of you have offered to purchase the entire amount of McBonds and at attractive prices. This blows my mind! After averaging the bids, we have selected the price of one hundred dollars per McBond, which yields an attractive 6 percent tax-free. As stated before, the minimum number of McBonds that can be purchased will be ten or $1,000. It never dawned on us to set a maximum. However, the maximum amount of McBonds that can be purchased will be one hundred or $10,000. I hope everyone understands and that those of you who wanted to purchase more will still be interested in purchasing one hundred."

Everyone in the room stands up and applauds. I'm happy because we are getting our washing machines and dryers. I'm also getting twenty dollars per month tax-free to spend at McDonalds for the reasonable price of $4,000, which is exactly what I wanted. I can understand why the attorneys at HQ might have been concerned. They are probably used to

116

dealing with greedy people of low character. Legally speaking, perhaps the highest bidders should have been able to purchase all the McBonds, leaving out the small bidders, but that would have defeated a major purpose of the program, which is to reward the volunteers.

Fortunately, this is a group of good-hearted, giving, and loving people. I would be shocked if there are any issues with the decisions Marge and her superiors have arrived at. May God bless Ronald McDonald House Charities and all who require their services as well as all the paid and volunteer staff.

EPILOGUE

It's been a few years since I volunteered at Ronald McDonald House Charities and several years since I took my introductory tour. The story about the washers, dryers, widgets, and McBonds is fictional and for illustrative purposes only. The other stories represent true situations that are sometimes blended, and the names are changed.

I attempted to keep this narrative brief and explain important personal financial basics to those who do "real work" in a format that is easy to understand. I encourage you to establish an emergency fund and, if you owe money on a home, to get a copy of the mortgage amortization schedule from the lender. If you have a mortgage with a variable interest rate, consider refinancing with a fixed rate.

I recommend visiting the websites listed. Consider subscribing to *Kiplinger's Personal Finance Magazine.* If you do not have a computer, most libraries have one that you can use, and someone can help you get started. You can request mutual fund or brokerage enrollment forms by phone or print them at the library and complete them at home. Mail the completed form in with your initial deposit. It's that simple!

I would like to leave you with the words of William Arthur Ward: "The pessimist complains about the wind, the optimist expects it to change, and the realist adjusts the sails."

God bless, and best wishes for hitting your tipping point in the near future.

fidelity.com

troweprice.com

ishares.com

vanguard.com

seekingalpha.com

morningstar.com

scottrade.com

dripinvesting.org

dividendyieldhunter.com

wealthtrack.com

federalreserve.gov

ABOUT THE AUTHOR

Marvin L. Piersall is enjoying early retirement from a suc-
cessful career as program planner for the Bureau of
Financial Policy Research and Analysis. He earned an asso-
ciate of arts degree in business administration from Lincoln
Land Community College and a bachelor of arts degree in
management from the University of Illinois at Springfield.
He performed economic research at the Bureau of the
Budget during his senior year of college. While serving in

the United States Navy and living across the street from a marina, he met a forty-year-old retired investor who ended up having a major impact on his life.

Piersall purchased his first house when he was twenty-two and continued to purchase properties, study investments, and question everyone he met who had achieved early retirement. Today, he provides others with personal finance advice so that they can do the same.

APPENDIX

First of Month	Monthly Interest	Monthly Contribution	End-of-Month Balance
$3,000	.005	Last day of month	Total
(1) $3,000	$15	$100	$3,115
(2) $3,115	$15.57	$100	$3,230.57
(3) $3,230.57	$16.15	$100	$3,346.72
(4) $3,346.72	$16.73	$100	$3,463.45
(5) $3,463.45	$17.32	$100	$3,580.77
(6) $3,580.77	$17.90	$100	$3,698.67
(7) $3,698.67	$18.49	$100	$3,835.65
(8) $3,835.65	$19.18	$100	$3,954.83
(9) $3,954.83	$19.77	$100	$4,074.60
(10) $4,074.60	$20.37	$100	$4,194.97
(11) $4,194.97	$20.97	$100	$4,315.94
(12) $4,315.94	$21.58	$100	$4,437.52
(13) $4,437.52	$22.19	$100	$4,559.71
(14) $4,559.71	$22.80	$100	$4,682.51
(15) $4,682.51	$23.41	$100	$4,805.92
(16) $4,805.92	$24.03	$100	$4,929.95
(17) $4,929.95	$24.65	$100	$5,054.60
(18) $5,054.60	$25.27	$100	$5,179.87
(19) $5,179.87	$25.90	$100	$5,305.77
(20) $5,305.77	$26.53	$100	$5,432.30
(21) $5,432.30	$27.16	$100	$5,559.46
(22) $5,559.46	$27.80	$100	$5,687.26
(23) $5,687.26	$28.44	$100	$5,815.70

(24) $5,815.70	$29.08	$100	$5,944.78
(25) $5,944.78	$29.72	$100	$6,074.50
(26) $6,074.50	$30.37	$100	$6,204.87
(27) $6,204.87	$31.02	$100	$6,335.89
(28) $6,335.89	$31.68	$100	$6,467.57
(29) $6,467.57	$32.34	$100	$6,599.91
(30) $6,599.91	$33.00	$100	$6,732.91
(31) $6,732.91	$33.66	$100	$6,866.57
(32) $6,866.57	$34.33	$100	$7,000.90
(33) $7,000.90	$35.00	$100	$7,135.90
(34) $7,135.90	$35.68	$100	$7,271.58
(35) $7,271.58	$36.36	$100	$7,407.94
(36) $7,407.94	$37.04	$100	$7,544.98
(37) $7,544.98	$37.72	$100	$7,682.70
(38) $7,682.7	$38.41	$100	$7,821.11
(39) $7,821.11	$39.11	$100	$7,960.22
(40) $7,960.22	$39.80	$100	$8,100.02
(41) $8,100.02	$40.50	$100	$8,240.52
(42) $8,240.52	$41.20	$100	$8,381.72
(43) $8,381.72	$41.91	$100	$8,523.63
(44) $8,523.63	$42.62	$100	$8,666.25
(45) $8,666.25	$43.33	$100	$8,809.58
(46) $8,809.58	$44.05	$100	$8,953.63
(47) $8,953.63	$44.77	$100	$9,098.40
(48) $9,098.40	$45.49	$100	$9,243.89
(49) $9,243.89	$46.22	$100	$9,390.11
(50) $9,390.11	$46.95	$100	$9,537.06
(51) $9,537.06	$47.69	$100	$9,684.75
(52) $9,684.75	$48.42	$100	$9,833.17
(53) $9,833.17	$49.17	$100	$9,982.34
(54) $9,982.34	$49.91	$100	$10,132.25
(55) $10,132.25	$50.66	$100	$10,282.91
(56) $10,282.91	$51.41	$100	$10,434.32
(57) $10,434.32	$52.17	$100	$10,586.49
(58) $10,586.49	$52.93	$100	$10,739.42
(59) $10,739.42	$53.70	$100	$10,893.12

(60) $10,893.12	$54.47	$100	$11,047.59
(61) $11,047.59	$55.24	$100	$11,202.83
(62) $11,202.83	$56.01	$100	$11,358.84
(63) $11,358.84	$56.79	$100	$11,515.63
(64) $11,515.63	$57.58	$100	$11,673.21
(65) $11,673.21	$58.37	$100	$11,889.95
(66) $11,889.95	$59.45	$100	$12,049.4
(67) $12,049.40	$60.25	$100	$12,209.65
(68) $12,209.65	$61.05	$100	$12,370.70
(69) $12,370.70	$61.85	$100	$12,532.55
(70) $12,532.55	$62.66	$100	$12,695.21
(71) $12,695.21	$63.48	$100	$12,858.69
(72) $12,858.69	$64.29	$100	$13,022.98
(73) $13,022.98	$65.12	$100	$13,188.10
(74) $13,188.10	$65.94	$100	$13,354.04
(75) $13,354.04	$66.77	$100	$13,520.81
(76) $13,520.81	$67.60	$100	$13,688.41
(77) $13,688.41	$68.44	$100	$13,856.85
(78) $13,856.85	$69.28	$100	$13,926.13
(79) $13,926.13	$69.63	$100	$14,095.76
(80) $14,095.76	$70.48	$100	$14,266.24
(81) $14,266.24	$71.33	$100	$14,437.57
(82) $14,437.57	$72.19	$100	$14,609.76
(83) $14,609.76	$73.05	$100	$14,782.81
(84) $14,782.81	$73.91	$100	$14,956.72
(85) $14,956.72	$74.78	$100	$15,131.50
(86) $15,131.50	$75.66	$100	$15,307.16
(87) $15,307.16	$76.54	$100	$15,483.70
(88) $15,483.70	$77.42	$100	$15,661.12
(89) $15,661.12	$78.31	$100	$15,739.43
(90) $15,739.43	$78.70	$100	$15,818.13
(91) $15,818.13	$79.09	$100	$15,897.22
(92) $15,897.22	$79.49	$100	$16,076.71
(93) $16,076.71	$80.38	$100	$16,257.09
(94) $16,257.09	$81.29	$100	$16,438.38
(95) $16,438.38	$82.19	$100	$16,620.57

(96) $16,620.57	$83.10	$100	$16,803.67
(97) $16,803.67	$84.02	$100	$16,987.69
(98) $16,987.69	$84.94	$100	$17,172.63
(99) $17,172.63	$85.86	$100	$17,258.49
(100) $17,258.49	$86.29	$100	$17,444.78
(101) $17,444.78	$87.22	$100	$17,532.00
(102) $17,532.00	$87.66	$100	$17,719.66
(103) $17,719.66	$88.60	$100	$17,908.26
(104) $17,908.26	$89.54	$100	$17,997.80
(105) $17,997.80	$89.99	$100	$18,187.79
(106) $18,187.79	$90.94	$100	$18,378.73
(107) $18,378.73	$91.89	$100	$18,570.62
(108) $18,570.62	$92.85	$100	$18,663.47
(109) $18,663.47	$93.32	$100	$18,856.79
(110) $18,856.79	$94.28	$100	$18,951.07
(111) $18,951.07	$94.76	$100	$19,145.83
(112) $19,145.83	$95.73	$100	$19,341.56
(113) $19,341.56	$96.71	$100	$19,538.27
(114) $19,538.27	$97.69	$100	$19,735.96
(115) $19,735.96	$98.68	$100	$19,934.64
(116) $19,934.64	$99.67	$100	$20,134.31
(117) $20,134.31	$100.67	$100	$20,334.98
(118) $20,334.98	$101.67	$100	$20,536.65
(119) $20,536.65	$102.68	$100	$20,739.33
(120) $20,739.33	$103.70	$100	$20,943.03
(121) $20,943.03	$104.72	$100	$21,147.75
(122) $21,147.75	$105.74	$100	$21,353.49
(123) $21,353.49	$106.77	$100	$21,560.26
(124) $21,560.26	$107.80	$100	$21,768.06
(125) $21,768.06	$108.84	$100	$21,976.90
(126) $21,976.90	$109.88	$100	$22,186.78
(127) $22,186.78	$110.93	$100	$22,397.71
(128) $22,397.71	$111.99	$100	$22,609.70
(129) $22,609.70	$113.05	$100	$22,822.75
(130) $22,822.75	$114.11	$100	$23,036.86
(131) $23,036.86	$115.18	$100	$23,252.04

(132) $23,252.04	$116.26	$100	$23,468.30
(133) $23,468.30	$117.34	$100	$23,685.64
(134) $23,685.64	$118.43	$100	$23,904.07
(135) $23,904.07	$119.52	$100	$24,123.59
(136) $24,123.59	$120.62	$100	$24,344.21
(137) $24,344.21	$121.72	$100	$24,565.93
(138) $24,565.93	$122.83	$100	$24,788.76
(139) $24,788.76	$123.94	$100	$25,012.70
(140) $25,012.70	$125.06	$100	$25,237.76
(141) $25,237.76	$126.19	$100	$25,463.95
(142) $25,463.95	$127.32	$100	$25,691.27
(143) $25,691.27	$128.46	$100	$25,919.73
(144) $25,919.73	$129.60	$100	$26,149.33
(145) $26,149.33	$130.75	$100	$26,380.08
(146) $26,380.08	$131.90	$100	$26,611.98
(147) $26,611.98	$133.06	$100	$26,845.04
(148) $26,845.04	$134.23	$100	$27,079.27
(149) $27,079.27	$135.40	$100	$27,314.67
(150) $27,314.67	$136.57	$100	$27,551.24
(151) $27,551.24	$137.76	$100	$27,789.00
(152) $27,789.00	$138.95	$100	$28,027.95
(153) $28,027.95	$140.14	$100	$28,268.09
(154) $28,268.09	$141.34	$100	$28,509.43
(155) $28,509.43	$142.55	$100	$28,751.98
(156) $28,751.98	$143.76	$100	$28,995.74
(157) $28,995.74	$144.98	$100	$29,240.72
(158) $29,240.72	$146.20	$100	$29,486.92
(159) $29,486.92	$147.43	$100	$29,734.35
(160) $29,734.35	$148.67	$100	$29,983.02
(161) $29,983.02	$149.92	$100	$30,232.94
(162) $30,232.94	$151.16	$100	$30,484.10
(163) $30,484.10	$152.42	$100	$30,736.52
(164) $30,736.52	$153.68	$100	$30,990.20
(165) $30,990.20	$154.95	$100	$31,245.15
(166) $31,245.15	$156.23	$100	$31,501.38
(167) $31,501.38	$157.51	$100	$31,758.89

(168) $31,758.89	$158.79	$100	$31,917.68
(169) $31,917.68	$159.59	$100	$32,177.27
(170) $32,177.27	$160.89	$100	$32,438.16
(171) $32,438.16	$162.19	$100	$32,700.35
(172) $32,700.35	$163.50	$100	$32,963.85
(173) $32,963.85	$164.82	$100	$33,228.67
(174) $33,228.67	$166.14	$100	$33,494.81
(175) $33,494.81	$167.47	$100	$33,762.28
(176) $33,762.28	$168.81	$100	$34,031.09
(177) $34,031.09	$170.16	$100	$34,301.25
(178) $34,301.25	$171.51	$100	$34,572.76
(179) $34,572.76	$172.86	$100	$34,848.62
(180) $34,848.62	$174.24	$100	$35,122.86
(181) $35,122.86	$175.61	$100	$35,398.47
(182) $35,398.47	$176.99	$100	$35,675.46
(183) $35,675.46	$178.38	$100	$35,953.84
(184) $35,953.84	$179.77	$100	$36,233.61
(185) $36,233.61	$181.17	$100	$36,514.78
(186) $36,514.78	$182.57	$100	$36,697.35
(187) $36,697.35	$183.49	$100	$36,980.84
(188) $36,980.84	$184.90	$100	$37,265.74
(189) $37,265.74	$186.33	$100	$37,552.07
(190) $37,552.07	$187.76	$100	$37,839.83
(191) $37,839.83	$189.20	$100	$38,129.03
(192) $38,129.03	$190.65	$100	$38,419.68
(193) $38,419.68	$192.10	$100	$38,711.78
(194) $38,711.78	$193.56	$100	$39,005.34
(195) $39,005.34	$195.03	$100	$39,300.37
(196) $39,300.37	$196.50	$100	$39,596.87
(197) $39,596.87	$197.98	$100	$39,894.85
(198) $39,894.85	$199.47	$100	$40,194.32
(199) $40,194.32	$200.97	$100	$40,495.29
(200) $40,495.29	$202.48	$100	$40,797.77
(201) $40,797.77	$203.99	$100	$41,101.76
(202) $41,101.76	$205.51	$100	$41,407.27
(203) $41,407.27	$207.04	$100	$41,714.31

(204) $41,714.31	$208.57	$100	$42,022.88
(205) $42,022.88	$210.11	$100	$42,332.99
(206) $42,332.99	$211.66	$100	$42,644.65
(207) $42,644.65	$213.22	$100	$42,957.87
(208) $42,957.87	$214.79	$100	$43,272.66
(209) $43,272.66	$216.36	$100	$43,589.02
(210) $43,589.02	$217.95	$100	$43,906.97
(211) $43,906.97	$219.53	$100	$44,226.50
(212) $44,226.50	$221.13	$100	$44,547.63
(213) $44,547.63	$222.74	$100	$44,870.37
(214) $44,870.37	$224.35	$100	$45,194.72
(215) $45,194.72	$225.97	$100	$45,520.69
(216) $45,520.69	$227.60	$100	$45,848.29
(217) $45,848.29	$229.24	$100	$46,177.53
(218) $46,177.53	$230.89	$100	$46,508.42
(219) $46,508.42	$232.54	$100	$46,840.96
(220) $46,840.96	$234.20	$100	$47,175.16
(221) $47,175.16	$235.88	$100	$47,511.04
(222) $47,511.04	$237.56	$100	$47,848.60
(223) $47,848.60	$239.24	$100	$48,187.84
(224) $48,187.84	$240.94	$100	$48,528.78
(225) $48,528.78	$242.64	$100	$48,871.42
(226) $48,871.42	$244.36	$100	$49,215.78
(227) $49,215.78	$246.08	$100	$49,561.86
(228) $49,561.86	$247.81	$100	$49,909.67
(229) $49,909.67	$249.55	$100	$50,259.22
(230) $50,259.22	$251.30	$100	$50,610.52
(231) $50,610.52	$253.05	$100	$50,963.57
(232) $50,963.57	$254.82	$100	$51,318.39
(233) $51,318.39	$256.59	$100	$51,674.98
(234) $51,674.98	$258.37	$100	$52,033.35
(235) $52,033.35	$260.17	$100	$52,393.52
(236) $52,393.52	$261.97	$100	$52,655.49
(237) $52,655.49	$263.28	$100	$53,018.77
(238) $53,018.77	$265.09	$100	$53,383.86
(239) $53,383.86	$266.92	$100	$53,750.78

(240) $53,750.78	$268.75	$100	$54,119.53
(241) $54,119.53	$270.60	$100	$54,490.13
(242) $54,490.13	$272.45	$100	$54,862.58
(243) $54,862.58	$274.31	$100	$55,236.89
(244) $55,236.89	$276.18	$100	$55,613.07
(245) $55,613.07	$278.07	$100	$55,991.14
(246) $55,991.14	$279.96	$100	$56,371.10
(247) $56,371.10	$281.86	$100	$56,752.96
(248) $56,752.96	$283.76	$100	$57,136.72
(249) $57,136.72	$285.68	$100	$57,522.40
(250) $57,522.40	$287.61	$100	$57,910.01
(251) $57,910.01	$289.55	$100	$58,299.56
(252) $58,299.56	$291.50	$100	$58,691.06
(253) $58,691.06	$293.46	$100	$59,084.52
(254) $59,084.52	$295.42	$100	$59,379.94
(255) $59,379.94	$296.90	$100	$59,776.84
(256) $59,776.84	$298.88	$100	$60,175.72
(257) $60,175.72	$300.88	$100	$60,576.60
(258) $60,576.60	$302.88	$100	$60,979.48
(259) $60,979.48	$304.90	$100	$61,384.38
(260) $61,384.38	$306.92	$100	$61,791.30
(261) $61,791.30	$308.96	$100	$62,200.26
(262) $62,200.26	$311.00	$100	$62,611.26
(263) $62,611.26	$313.06	$100	$63,024.32
(264) $63,024.32	$315.12	$100	$63,439.44
(265) $63,439.44	$317.20	$100	$63,856.64
(266) $63,856.64	$318.28	$100	$64,274.92
(267) $64,274.92	$321.37	$100	$64,696.29
(268) $64,696.29	$323.48	$100	$65,119.77
(269) $65,119.77	$325.60	$100	$65,545.37
(270) $65,545.37	$327.73	$100	$65,973.10
(271) $65,973.10	$329.87	$100	$66,402.97
(272) $66,402.97	$332.01	$100	$66,834.98
(273) $66,834.98	$334.17	$100	$67,269.15
(274) $67,269.15	$336.35	$100	$67,705.50
(275) $67,705.50	$338.53	$100	$68,144.03

(276) $68,144.03	$340.72	$100	$68,584.75
(277) $68,584.75	$342.92	$100	$69,027.67
(278) $69,027.67	$345.14	$100	$69,472.81
(279) $69,472.81	$347.36	$100	$69,920.17
(280) $69,920.17	$349.60	$100	$70,369.77
(281) $70,369.77	$351.85	$100	$70,821.62
(282) $70,821.62	$354.11	$100	$71,275.73
(283) $71,275.73	$356.38	$100	$71,732.11
(284) $71,732.11	$358.66	$100	$72,190.77
(285) $72,190.77	$360.95	$100	$72,651.72
(286) $72,651.72	$363.26	$100	$73,114.98
(287) $73,114.98	$365.57	$100	$73,580.55
(288) $73,580.55	$367.90	$100	$74,048.45
(289) $74,048.45	$370.24	$100	$74,518.69
(290) $74,518.69	$372.59	$100	$74,991.28
(291) $74,991.28	$374.96	$100	$75,466.24
(292) $75,466.24	$377.93	$100	$75,944.17
(293) $75,944.17	$379.72	$100	$76,423.89
(294) $76,423.89	$382.12	$100	$76,906.01
(295) $76,906.01	$384.53	$100	$77,390.54
(296) $77,390.54	$386.95	$100	$77,877.49
(297) $77,877.49	$389.39	$100	$78,366.88
(298) $78,366.88	$391.83	$100	$78,858.71
(299) $78,858.71	$394.29	$100	$79,353.00
(300) $79,353.00	$396.77	$100	$79,849.77
(301) $79,849.77	$399.25	$100	$80,349.02
(302) $80,349.02	$401.75	$100	$80,850.77
(303) $80,850.77	$404.25	$100	$81,355.02
(304) $81,355.02	$406.78	$100	$81,861.80
(305) $81,861.80	$409.31	$100	$82,371.11
(306) $82,371.11	$411.86	$100	$82,882.97
(307) $82,882.97	$414.41	$100	$83,397.38
(308) $83,397.38	$416.99	$100	$83,914.37
(309) $83,914.37	$419.57	$100	$84,433.94
(310) $84,433.94	$422.17	$100	$84,956.11
(311) $84,956.11	$424.78	$100	$85,480.89

(312) $85,480.89	$427.40	$100	$86,008.29
(313) $86,008.29	$430.04	$100	$86,538.33
(314) $86,538.33	$432.69	$100	$87,071.02
(315) $87,071.02	$435.36	$100	$87,606.38
(316) $87,606.38	$438.03	$100	$88,144.41
(317) $88,144.41	$440.72	$100	$88,685.13
(318) $88,685.13	$443.43	$100	$89,228.56
(319) $89,228.56	$446.14	$100	$89,774.70
(320) $89,774.70	$448.87	$100	$90,323.57
(321) $90,323.57	$451.62	$100	$90,875.19
(323) $90,875.19	$454.38	$100	$91,429.57
(324) $91,429.57	$457.15	$100	$91,986.72
(325) $91,986.72	$459.93	$100	$92,546.65
(326) $92,546.65	$462.73	$100	$93,109.38
(327) $93,109.38	$465.55	$100	$93,674.93
(328) $93,674.93	$468.37	$100	$94,243.30
(329) $94,243.30	$471.22	$100	$94,814.52
(330) $94,814.52	$474.07	$100	$95,388.59
(331) $95,388.59	$476.94	$100	$95,965.53
(332) $95,965.53	$479.83	$100	$96,545.36
(333) $96,545.36	$482.73	$100	$97,128.09
(334) $97,128.09	$485.64	$100	$97,713.73
(335) $97,713.73	$488.57	$100	$98,302.30
(336) $98,302.30	$491.51	$100	$98,893.81
(337) $98,893.81	$494.47	$100	$99,488.28
(338) $99,488.28	$497.44	$100	$100,085.72
(339) $100,085.72	$500.43	$100	$100,686.15
(340) $100,686.15	$503.43	$100	$101,289.58
(341) $101,289.58	$506.45	$100	$101,896.03
(342) $101,896.03	$509.48	$100	$102,505.51
(343) $102,505.51	$512.53	$100	$103,118.04
(344) $103,118.04	$515.59	$100	$103,733.63
(345) $103,733.63	$518.67	$100	$104,352.3
(346) $104,352.3	$521.76	$100	$104,974.06
(347) $104,974.06	$524.87	$100	$105,598.93
(348) $105,598.93	$527.99	$100	$106,226.92

(349) $106,226.92	$531.13	$100	$106,858.05
(350) $106,858.05	$534.29	$100	$107,492.34
(351) $107,492.34	$537.46	$100	$108,129.8
(352) $108,129.8	$540.65	$100	$108,770.45
(353) $108,770.45	$543.85	$100	$109,414.3
(354) $109,414.3	$547.07	$100	$110,061.37
(355) $110,061.37	$550.31	$100	$110,711.68
(356) $110,711.68	$553.56	$100	$111,365.24
(357) $111,365.24	$556.83	$100	$112,022.07
(358) $112,022.07	$560.11	$100	$112,682.18
(359) $112,682.18	$563.41	$100	$113,345.59
(360) $113,345.59	$566.73	$100	$114,012.32

BIBLIOGRAPHY

Fidelity "How to efficiently turn savings into income" *Fidelity Viewpoints* July 24, 2013 https://www.fidelity.com/viewpoints/retirement/savings-to-income

Fidelity "Safeguard your retirement income" *Fidelity Viewpoints* June 26, 2013 www.fidelity.com/viewpoints/retirement/safeguard-retirement-savings

Gambardello, Joseph A. "In Harrowing High-seas Rescue, Tugboat Crew Pulled To Safety An Aircraft Carrier Found The Eight, Who Had Abandoned Ship. Three Of Them Floated In Lifejackets For 5 ½ Hours" *The Inquirer* September 16, 1999 http://articles.philly.com/1999-09-16/news/25488832_1_aircraft-carrier-high-seas-rescue-flight-deck.

Kristof, Kathy. "History Says Stick With Stocks" *Kiplinger's Personal Finance* August 2013

Mack, Consuelo. "Benz & Kinnel" *WEALTHTRACK* November 15, 2013 http://wealthtrack.com/recent-programs/benz-kinnel-mutual-fund-shakeups/

Mack, Consuelo. "Cortazzo & Lebenthal Minimizing Tax Pain" *WEALTHTRACK* December 13, 2013 http://wealthtrack.

com/recent-programs/premium-mark-cortazzo-alexandra-lebenthal-2/

T. Rowe Price Report "Bond Strategies for Rising Interest Rates" Issue 120 Summer 2013 http://individual.troweprice.com/staticFiles/Retail/Shared/PDFs/Summer2013PriceReport.pdf

Thomas, Brad. "Is Now The Time To Double Down In REIT Town?" *Seeking Alpha* August 19, 2013 http://seekingalpha.com/article/1643042-is-now-the-time-to-double-down-in-reit-town

Van Deventer, Donald. "Straight Talk: 6 Candid Rules For Individual Investors" *Seeking Alpha* August 29, 2013 http://seekingalpha.com/article/1665572-straight-talk-6-candid-rules-for-individual-investors

Van Knapp, David. "Bogle's Views on Retirement Income" *Seeking Alpha* July 18, 2013 http://seekingalpha.com/article/1556142-bogles-views-on-retirement-income

Yahoo Finance "Five Year Interactive Chart T. Rowe Price Tax-Free High Yield (PRFHX)" accessed Aug 6, 2013 http://finance.yahoo.com/echarts?s=PRFHX+Interactive#symbol=PRFHX;range=5y